This Day

This Day

A Wesleyan Way of Prayer

Laurence Hull Stookey

ABINGDON PRESS / Nashville

THIS DAY
A WESLEYAN WAY OF PRAYER

Copyright © 2004 by Abingdon Press

All rights reserved.

No part of this work may be reproduced or transmitted in any form or by any means, electronic or mechanical, including photocopying and recording, or by any information storage or retrieval system, except as may be expressly permitted by the 1976 Copyright Act or in writing from the publisher. Requests for permission should be addressed to Abingdon Press, P.O. Box 801, 201 Eighth Avenue South, Nashville, TN 37202-0801 or permissions@abingdonpress.com

This book is printed on elemental-chlorine–free paper.

ISBN-13: 978-0-687-07486-0

Permissions continued on p. 216.

07 08 09 10 11 12 13—10 9 8 7 6 5 4 3 2

MANUFACTURED IN THE UNITED STATES OF AMERICA

Contents

Preface 9

Introduction 13
   Scope of the Book 13
   Design of the Book 15
   The Daily Order and How to Use It 17
   Commentary on Components of the Daily Order 18
   A Theological Postscript: The Interaction of Corporate Worship
     and Personal Prayer 25

I. The Daily Order 27

II. Acts Appropriate to the Day of the Week 103
   The Lord's Day 103
   Monday 103
   Tuesday 104
   Wednesday 105
   Thursday 105
   Friday 106
   Saturday 106

III. Acts Appropriate to the Time of the Year 107
   The Church's Year
     Advent
     Introduction 107
     Prayers for Advent 107
     Advent and Christian Hope 108
     The Hectic Pace of Advent as a Call to Confession 109

Christmas
Introduction 110
Meditations for Christmas 111
Prayer for the Season of Christmas 111
For Meditation and Confession at Christmas 112
Christmas Poem: "A Child My Choice" 113
Christmas Poem: "Thou Didst Leave Thy Throne" 114
Silence in Heaven: An Imaginative Account 115

The Epiphany and Baptism of the Lord
Introduction 117
A Prayer for the Epiphany 117
Prayer for the Sunday of the Lord's Baptism 118

Lent
Introduction 118
A Prayer for Use Throughout Lent 118
Prayer for Ash Wednesday 119
An Ash Wednesday Meditation 120
A Poem for Holy Week: "My Song Is Love Unknown" . . 121
A Prayer for Palm-Passion Sunday 122
A Prayer for Holy Thursday 123
A Prayer for Good Friday 123
A Prayer for the Eve of Easter 124

Easter: The Great Fifty Days
Introduction 124
An Address to Death 125
A Meditation on the New Life in Christ 125
A Prayer During the Great Fifty Days 126
A Prayer for Ascension Day 127
A Prayer for the Day of Pentecost 127
A Meditaton on the Varying Ministries of the
    Holy Spirit 127

Other Occasions of the Church's Year
A Prayer for Trinity Sunday 128
A Prayer for All Saints' Day 129
A Prayer for the Sunday of Christ's Reign 129

The Civil Year

    At the Opening of a New Calendar Year 130

    For Martin Luther King, Jr., Day 130

    For National Holidays 131

    On Days Honoring Parents or Grandparents 132

    At the Beginning of a New School Year 133

    For Thanksgiving Day 133

IV. Acts Appropriate to the Occasion 135

    In Times of Distress, Illness, and Death

    For the Sick and Those Who Minister to Them 135

    In Times of Great Distress Due to Natural Disaster

      or Humanly Devised Evil 136

    For Those with Mental Illness 137

    When You Are Seriously Ill 138

    Thanksgiving after Recovery from an Illness 138

    When Your Own Death Seems Imminent 139

    For Any Who Watch with Those to Whom Death

      Draws Near 141

    When Mourning the Loss of a Friend 141

    For the Bereaved 142

    Concerning the Life and Mission of the Church

    For Your Own Congregation 142

    Before a Congregational Business Meeting 143

    For the Lay Leadership of the Church 143

    For the Clergy Leadership of the Church 143

    For Those Being Ordained 144

    For Bishops and Other Leaders of the Church 144

    For the Legislative Bodies of the Church 145

    For the Courts of the Church 146

    For the Unity of the Church Universal 147

    For a Just and Compassionate Society

    For God's Help in Alleviating Injustice 147

    For Freedom from Racial Prejudice 148

    For Those Who Know the Sting of Discrimination 149

    To Be Led in the Ways of Justice and Peace 149

    For Justice in Our Communities and the World 150

    For the Future 150

In the Struggle for Truth 150
For Those Who Grow Weary in the Struggle
    for Justice 151

Prayers for Times of the Day
Morning 152
Midday 152
Evening 153

Other Resources
A Centering Prayer 153
A Prayer to the Holy Spirit 154
Before Reading the Scriptures 154
Discipleship 154
Divine Love 155
For Spiritual Concentration 155
A Student's Prayer 156
The Lord's Prayer: Current Ecumenical Text 156
The Lord's Prayer: A Traditional Text 157
The Lord's Prayer: Another Traditional Text 157
The Apostles' Creed 157
The Nicene Creed 158

V. Personal Prayer Surrounding the Congregational Service 159

VI. Use of the Psalms in Times of Trouble and Terror 165

VII. Teaching Children to Pray 173

VIII. Lectionary 179

Preface

This is a book I never intended to write. For me, the gestation period for a book is exceedingly long—about a decade in the thought process, at a minimum. Constructing a book of daily devotions was a possibility that had never entered my mind until I received a phone call from my denomination's publishing house, imploring me to take on just such a task. Their deadline for my manuscript was only eighteen months off, and I told the caller bluntly that in the midst of a very hectic academic schedule, I would not even have time to think about the book until my sabbatical leave began almost a year later. Against my better judgment I agreed to take the assignment, however.

Of course I did think about the book long before sabbatical leave began, largely to fuss endlessly with myself over my inability to say no to a project I really did not wish to do. But often we find that with great benefit in the end, God pushes us in directions we have no desire to go. As I pondered the project further, the persistent question in my mind was: "What fresh ways are there to design a book of daily prayer? What, if anything, can I do that has not been done many times before?"

I proceeded by identifying my own gripes with prayer guides that I have tried and often put aside as not workable for me. Wherein was my discontent? I identified three areas. The first two are practical, even mechanical; the third is deeply theological.

(1) There is a vast array of small booklet types of daily devotions, each about a page in length and five or so minutes in duration. The brevity seems to trivialize daily prayer, making it like a brief greeting exchanged with God on the street in passing, rather than any sustained conversation with the One who loves us and continually offers us great grace. The daily orders in *This Day* cannot be done with integrity in so short a time. If you wish for very brief devotions, this book will not meet your needs.

(2) Most daily prayer books print everything needed for that day on consecutive pages. This makes for great convenience but no flexibility. In *This Day* on any given occasion you may wish to refer to several collections of resources that follow the thirty-one daily orders. It will take a bit of time to learn this system, but in the end the system will provide more opportunities for variety. If you want a book that does not require you to turn pages and use page markers, please look elsewhere.

(3) Most daily prayer books, even those produced as official resources by denominations, are largely individualistic. This reinforces the prevailing notion that daily devotions are "my time alone with my God." One would never know from looking at these guides to prayer that actual congregations exist and that these are gathered into actual denominations. How odd, since the New Testament is determinedly "churchy." Possibly the only book therein written to an individual rather than a congregation or the pastor of a congregation is little Philemon. The Gospel of Luke and its companion volume, the Acts, are addressed to "Theophilus," who may have been an individual. But the name (which translates as "Lover of God") may as readily refer to a group: Any who love God are to be edified by reading these two books. Therefore a careful use of *This Day* will force you to think about your life within a congregation and will require you to pray for your own local worshiping community as well as your denomination and the "holy catholic church" that lies beyond it. If you are seeking devotions directed only to your personal needs, and prayers only for your close friends and family, this book will not please you.

Have I given you by now enough reasons not to use *This Day?* I hope not, because I want to believe that you are up to the challenge of a daily prayer guide that is a bit unusual, that stretches its users and strengthens spiritual muscles that may now lie dormant.

Suffice it to say that once I got to the work of writing this book, I became increasingly excited about its design and possibilities. I think there are some things about it that are fresh and enlivening, and I hope you will find it to be so as well. Yes, it would be a much stronger book had I had opportunity to "let it simmer" in my mind for a decade before putting ink to paper. Possibly ten years from now I will write a superior successor.

Until then, I wish for all of us growth in grace and strength for service in the name of the Lord Jesus.

> *Laurence Hull Stookey*
> *Professor of Preaching and Worship,*
> *Wesley Theological Seminary*
> *Pastor, Asbury United Methodist Church,*
> *Allen, Maryland*

Introduction

Scope of the Book

This Day is intended for those who want a once-a-day devotional guide that can be used for a period of fifteen to twenty minutes. The time of day at which you use the book is up to you. Unlike some classic prayer books, this book does not contain separate prayer services for morning and evening or other specified hours. Some who use *This Day* will use it at a regularly appointed time, be that morning, noon, early evening, or bedtime. Others may vary the time from day to day, especially on weekends. It is intended that you should do what works for you, without being intimidated by patterns others find useful for themselves.

This book was commissioned by The United Methodist Publishing House as a part of its denominational resources. Still, it is intended for use beyond the confines of one particular denomination. The Methodist movement did not invent prayer; nor is there a distinctively "Wesleyan way" of praying. The Wesleyan aspect of this book lies more in its basic assumptions than in the actual form of its prayers. Wesleyans seek to balance corporate and individual expressions of love for God and love for neighbor. In an attempt to achieve this balance, we have devised the following formula, which is reflected in *This Day*:

Acts of Piety (Love for God)
> Congregational worship and study, including the appropriation of the Sacraments.
> Private prayer and study, fasting, and personal disciplines that focus on divine grace.

Acts of Charity (Love for Neighbor)
>Seeking social justice through legislation and civic involvement to effect reform in our world.
>Doing acts of compassion toward those who are suffering, especially those discriminated against and all persons who are in need because societal reform has not yet been sufficiently achieved.

The content of this formula is by no means unique to Methodists, but this particular way of organizing that content may be something we Wesleyans have to share with other branches of the church. We think that this way of approaching discipleship gives us a readily remembered manner of self-assessment as we seek to "go on to perfection" in the pursuit of Matthew 5:48. (For elaboration on this point, seek the material for Day 5, p. 37.)

While *This Day* is therefore intended to be suitable for persons in many denominations it is specifically designed for those who are active members of a local Christian congregation. Far from being a book to be used instead of attending congregational services of worship, it is intentionally geared toward those who attend regularly or who earnestly wish to attend but are prevented by physical impairment, work schedules, or other unavoidable impediments.

Because prayer needs to be as concrete as possible, there are prayers that are specifically United Methodist in scope, or at least broadly Methodist (including African Methodist Episcopal, African Methodist Episcopal Zion, British Methodist, Christian Methodist Episcopal, Free Methodist, Wesleyan Methodist). For example, there are specific prayers for bishops, Judicial Council, district superintendents or presiding elders, and so on. Exact designations vary within the Wesleyan family of churches. Those outside of that family may find exact wording a bit unfamiliar, but likely they can at least be reminded of their own governmental structures and personnel that are in need of prayer, even if they do not use terms such as "bishop," "jurisdictional conference," or "general boards and agencies." The use of these denominationally specific items is confined to the section Acts Appropriate to the Occasion, however, and can be passed over, or adapted as necessary by those outside of The United Methodist Church who wish to use this book.

Some may inquire as to why 366 daily orders are not provided, rather than only thirty-one. Does this not consign us to a monthly repetition of prayers and psalms? Yes, but such repetition has great strengths that often go unrecognized. Repetition results in memorization. Particularly in times of distress, we call up for use from our memories texts we may not even know we have learned. In the past several decades any number of hostages and prisoners of war who have been held in isolation with no access to books, and sometimes in darkness, have reported the same experience: What kept them sane was their ability to quote the Scriptures, the prayers, and the hymns of their religious traditions. When we have no access to liturgical books, through our memories God may give us great strength in the time of testing.

Design of the Book

Section I. The Daily Order

Thirty-one daily orders are provided, corresponding to the calendar days of each month. Day 1 invites you to look ahead into the month just beginning, to anticipate its challenges and opportunities, and to set spiritual goals for yourself. The order headed "Final Day" is used on the final day of the month and gives you an opportunity to review the month now ending, to give thanks for its blessings and to seek forgiveness for wrongs you have committed and for your neglect of the good you might have done.

Variety is achieved not by changing the sequence of events drastically from one day to the next but by inserting into a uniform structure readings, prayers, and other acts

    (a) appropriate to the day of the week,

    (b) related to the time of the year, and

    (c) suitable to the needs of a particular day.

These resources are arranged accordingly to form Sections II, III, and IV, outlined below.

The Daily Order section is found on pages 27-102.

Section II. Acts Appropriate to the Day of the Week

Certain types of daily devotion are appropriate to the day of the week on which we pray, regardless of the day of the month on which this falls. In particular:

- Friday historically has been a time to remember our redemption by Christ, which we mark annually with Good Friday, but which also can be recalled with benefit weekly.
- Saturday is a time to prepare ourselves for participation in congregational worship on Sunday. More is said on pages 25-26 about the relation between the prayer of the congregation gathered for worship and the daily prayer of individual members of the congregation scattered for service in the world.
- Sunday since earliest times has been more correctly called the Lord's Day: the day claimed as his own by the Lord Jesus, who on this day rose from the dead and fifty days later constituted the church by the power of the Holy Spirit.
- Monday is a time to reflect on what happened in congregational worship on the Lord's Day and to commit ourselves to the ministries assigned to us by God in carrying out the mission of the congregation.

On any date within the month you may insert into the daily order your choice of appropriate materials found in the Acts Appropriate to the Day of the Week section, pages 103-6.

Section III. Acts Appropriate to the Time of the Year

Certain events occur annually, not monthly, but surely are called to mind on appropriate days. In December, obviously we want to incorporate into the order for Day 25 the theme of our Lord's Nativity. In certain years Day 25 of March is Palm-Passion Sunday, Holy Thursday, Good Friday, or Easter Day. In some years, for those who live in the United States, Day 25 of May is Memorial Day, or Day 25 of November is Thanksgiving Day. But during the remaining months, Day 25 may have no such special significance.

Thematic materials from Section III (pages 107-34) can be integrated into the daily orders of Section I, as is appropriate to a particular month. This allows the daily orders to relate to important church or secular observances, without the need for 365 or more daily forms of prayer.

Section IV. Acts Appropriate to the Occasion

On any day of any month, you may wish to use in the daily order a variety of general resources: readings, prayers, forms of meditation, acts of praise, and so on. The Acts Appropriate to the Occasion section provides a selection of such materials drawn from differing eras, cultures, and denominational traditions. The pages are numbered 135-58.

Some acts, such as creeds, can be used at any time. The use of other acts ("at a time of national or international crisis," "after the death of those close to you," "in the face of natural disaster," "during illness") will be determined not by dates on any calendar but by the emergence of needs within our world.

The Daily Order and How to Use It

Daily Heading

Each daily order is headed by the day of the month: Day 1, Day 2, and so on through Day 30; then follows a final order called "Final Day." For months having 31 days, use 1-30 and Final Day. For months having 30 days, use 1-29 and Final Day. During February, use 1-27 and Final Day; or during leap year use 1-28 and Final Day.

Theme of the Day

In order to provide a particular focus and also to provide movement throughout each month, a theme is provided for each day, as follows:

Day 1, as already noted, opens the month and provides opportunities to look ahead.

Days 2, 3, and 4 turn our attention to the triune God to whom we pray, the God whose central characteristic is divine love.

Day 5 deals with how we return love to this God as we strive toward more serious and effective discipleship.

Day 6 begins to answer the question "What does this loving God require of us?"

Days 7-14 take us through the gifts of the Spirit described in Galatians 5:22—joy, peace, patience, kindness, generosity, faithfulness, gentleness, self-control. (The first gift of the Spirit listed by Paul—love—was considered on Days 2-6.)

Day 15 affords opportunity for a mid-month assessment of our discipleship.

Days 16-23 take as their themes the eight Beatitudes of Jesus.

Day 24 introduces the theme of life in community (the church).

Days 25-28 consider the characteristics of the church listed in the Nicene Creed: one, holy, catholic, and apostolic.

Day 29 has as its theme our hope eternal.

Day 30 is a time for giving thanks for the past month.

Final Day provides occasion for reflection and assessment of our lives in Christ in the month just ended. Then on Day 1 we again look forward to a new month.

Under the designation of the day of the month appear one or two quotations from the Bible related to the theme of the day. Then, in italics, each day's theme is noted in a sentence or two. Finally, matters to ponder about the theme of the day are set forth in several paragraphs.

Note that we have not yet gotten into the actual order for the day. The Bible verses and the matters to ponder will, however, guide your thinking and praying as you work your way through the daily order, which will now be described item by item.

Commentary on Components of the Daily Order

Opening Prayer

A brief prayer related to the daily theme is provided for each day. Because some will use this book when praying in groups but others will be alone while using it, some prayers are written using plural pronouns and others use singular forms. If the style of prayer on a particular day does not suit your needs, feel free to adapt it to your situation. Note, however, that because Christ connects all Christians to all other Christians, plural language is appropriate even when praying in solitude. Indeed, almost always when alone we continue to use plural pronouns when saying the Lord's Prayer.

Centering

What begins in the opening prayer is intensified here. The goal is to center our attention on God and thus to set aside the distractions of daily life that often consume us. Although quiet and concentration are always a part of centering, beyond that individuals respond to various kinds of approaches, suggested below:

Auditory. Total silence is a time-honored approach to centering. Others may prefer music, especially where it is helpful to mask distracting external noises. Recorded music can be used or a familiar hymn tune can be hummed.

Kinesthetic. Any posture is appropriate for prayer, but some people have decided preferences, such as kneeling or standing. Some may be helped by engaging in dance-like movements or by lifting the arms heavenward, with palms open and up.

Hand gestures have often been found useful. There is the traditional positioning of the hands, steeple-like, as in the famous woodcut "Praying Hands" by Albrecht Dürer. Or hands may rest quietly in one's lap, folded or with palms open and up, as if ready to receive a gift.

A very ancient gesture is a bit challenging to learn, but comes quite easily and with great meaning once it is mastered. Proceed as follows:

• Raise your right hand, as you might when taking an oath.
• Curl down toward the palm your little, ring, and middle fingers.
• Point the index finger as straight upward as possible.
• Now rest the thumb against the edge of the ring finger that is closest to your face.

If you now look at your hand, working outward:

• The index finger looks like the Greek letter "I" [iota].
• The middle finger looks like our "C," actually a form of "S" [sigma] in Greek.
• The thumb and ring finger form what appears to us to be an "X" [chi in Greek].
• The little finger is also a "C" [sigma].

You now have within your hand the ancient monogram of the words Jesus Christ. "IC" are the first and final letters of the Greek name "Jesus" and "XC" are the first and final letters of the messianic title "Christos." In virtually every ancient icon of the Savior, even in his infancy, he extends his right hand in blessing using exactly this gesture, thus identifying himself and offering us his grace. As Christians we bear his name and appropriately use his monogram as a reminder to ourselves of who and whose we are.

Once you have mastered this gesture, you can use it in other contexts. You can place your hand on your lap, unnoticed by others, during a prayer or sermon in the Sunday service as a way of concentrating on the liturgical task. While walking to and from the communion rail, you can hold your hand downward at your side, but still in this position, in a manner that does not at all parade your piety before others, since no one is likely to take notice.

A final form of kinesthetic concentration is careful attention to the pattern of your breathing. Breathe deeply and slowly for several minutes. Pause after each exhalation. This tends to relax the body and to refocus the mind.

Olfactory. For some, the use of incense or other fragrant substance may enhance prayerful concentration.

Visual. Many find it helpful to focus attention on a cross or crucifix, a lighted candle, or a religious picture such as an icon. Note well that God cannot be depicted accurately by any artist, not even in the Second Person of the Trinity, for we have no historical information as to how Jesus looked; and many find it most effective to identify with him in terms of their own ethnic or cultural appearance. Orthodox Christians helpfully point out that an icon is not a picture to be looked at, but a window to be looked through into heaven. There are, however, those who find it most helpful to keep their eyes closed as a way of shutting out all visual stimulation.

You may do more than one of the above things at the same time, or you may engage in other practices more to your personal benefit. Some people find it easiest to do none of the above but simply to engage in mental concentration as a means of centering. Even so, it may be useful to focus on one word or image that speaks to you of God: Think continuously of a stream of flowing water, of a light, of a shepherd, or of an open door, for example. (These images call to mind respectively John 4:14, 8:12, and 10:14; and Revelation 3:20.)

Some individuals become centered more quickly than others, and most of us will find that the time needed varies from day to day. When praying in a group, someone will need to take the responsibility of ending the period of silence by moving on to the prayer before the reading of Scripture.

Prayer for Illumination

This brief prayer typically asks
> (a) that we may understand the Scriptures as God speaks to us through them, and
> (b) that we may respond to them in obedient gratitude,
> (c) by the grace of the Holy Spirit, who enlightens and empowers us.

See comments above ("Opening Prayer") concerning singular and plural language styles.

Psalm

For each day, two psalms or psalm portions are provided. Although you may read both if you wish, the first is intended for Year One and the second for Year Two. See page 179 concerning when each year begins. On Sundays continue in the same year you are using for weekdays.

Scripture Readings for the Day

Readings from the other sixty-five books of the Bible follow a two year pattern on Mondays through Saturdays and a three year pattern on Sundays. While this may be a bit confusing, it seems the best usage, since many preachers follow this three year lectionary system in their sermons.

On Sundays, you can either use the daily order before attending worship services, in which case the assigned readings prepare you for the sermon. More likely, on Sundays (probably in the evening) it is well to use the daily order after attending worship services; thus the readings may enable you to recall key portions of the sermon and to reflect on these.

The Tables of Readings for both the weekly and the Sunday cycles are found on pages 179-215. Please note that the psalms assigned are related to the theme of the day; but the other Bible readings (covering a full year, not merely a month) are independent of the thematic design of this book. Because the Bible has a certain internal consistency, on some occasions the two or three year lectionary systems may seem to suit the day precisely; at other times this will not be the case.

How many of the suggested readings you wish to use on a given day will depend upon your personal schedule and interest. Perhaps on Sundays, you will wish to use all of the suggested readings. But if the day's sermon elaborated on only one of the readings, and if you use *This Day* after attending that service, you may prefer to meditate only on that one reading in light of the preacher's interpretation of it. On the other hand, you may decide that the sermon sufficiently amplified one passage, and you want to concentrate on the passages the preacher did not cover. The choice is yours. On weekdays, if you do not wish to use all of the readings supplied, you may decide to read through a particular book of the Bible in sequence. During Advent, for example, you may elect in Year One to read only the Isaiah passages day after day and to save the Epistle and Gospel readings for use in other years. Do what makes sense to you.

When reading scripture aloud in a group, the reader does well to proceed more slowly than is generally the case. There is no sermon to interpret the readings. Therefore we need more time to absorb the content than may be true when a preacher later expounds on the texts.

When not in a group but alone, you may well read the passages very slowly, pausing at the end of a phrase, even repeating words or phrases that seem particularly pertinent. In this way, you are in fact praying the Scriptures. By way of illustration, consider this very familiar passage. Possible reader's responses appear in italics:

The Lord, *yes* the Lord, is my shepherd. *Indeed as a Christian who has read John 10, I know that it is* the Lord Jesus Christ, the Good Shepherd, *who is my shepherd. No other guide is reliable. None other is to be trusted fully.* The Lord is my shepherd.

I shall not want. *But I am always wanting things. Granted, I do not need them all, but neither does God give me all of them. What do these words mean?* I shall not want. *O God, give me strength to believe that when you withhold from me what I want, you nevertheless give me all that I require. Enable me to separate my superficial wants from my true needs, and to trust you at all times.* I shall not want.

And so on. Obviously this form of reading can consume a significant amount of time. You will not do it with every passage every day. But note it as a particularly effective way to deal with passages that are very familiar; for in the reading of passages we virtually know by heart, we tend to go on "automatic pilot," realizing at the end that we have not been paying attention at all.

Incidentally, in the world in which the Bible arose, silent reading of any kind was virtually unknown. Even a solitary reader spoke aloud all that was being read. Note that in Acts 8:30 Philip the deacon, upon meeting an Ethiopian in the desert, "heard him reading." That is, the Ethiopian, sitting alone in his chariot, was reading aloud. Because of this custom, the Scriptures were written to be heard more so than to be seen. You may therefore find it commendable (if a bit odd at first) to read aloud even when you alone will hear the sound of your voice.

Contemplation

Unless you have prayed the Scriptures while reading them, as suggested above, a period of silence is suggested here. Ponder what the biblical passages say about your own expressions of discipleship. What changes in your life do they suggest? What gifts from God do you need to seek to fulfill what God asks of you? Or what gifts that you already have need to be cultivated for more effective use? Do the passages suggest persons or causes for which prayers should be offered? Causes to which service should be given?

When *This Day* is used in small groups, group members may be invited to offer concise reflections on the Scriptures read. Brief insights or questions are appropriate, but it is by no means intended that anyone should offer extended comments, let alone a sermon-like presentation.

The period of contemplation is also a time to review the comments on the theme of the day found at the beginning of each day's order.

Acts Appropriate to the Day of the Week

As noted above, Section II (pages 103-6) contains prayers designed for particular weekdays, especially those that cluster around the Lord's Day. Select those useful for this occasion.

Acts Appropriate to the Time of the Year

As also noted above, Section III (pages 107-34) contains readings, prayers, and other acts designed for particular seasons or occasions of both the church's calendar and the civil calendar. Select any that are suited to an occasion.

Acts Appropriate to the Occasion

Here materials can be drawn from Section IV (pages 135-58). It is equally appropriate to use here extemporaneous prayers related to particular concerns of the day.

The Prayer of the Whole Church

The church across the centuries has prayed in many different ways, and has often been bitterly divided in its beliefs and practices. But if there is one act in which all Christians have joined since the earliest times, it is the prayer commonly known either as "The Lord's Prayer" or "The Our Father." The alternative title, "The Prayer of the Whole Church," reminds us that nothing of comparable size has been translated into so many languages or used by so many people. When we pray these words we join our voices to those of Christians of every era. But we also dare to hope for the reunion of all of Christ's people, so that the world may behold an undivided witness to the power and love of God made known in Jesus.

Two traditional forms of the prayer as well as the current ecumenical text are found on pages 156-57.

Closing

If a number of people pray together, they may exchange greetings of peace before or after someone within the group offers a word of blessing. If you are praying in solitude, you may close in any way you find suitable.

A Theological Postscript: The Interaction of Corporate Worship and Personal Prayer

Christianity is a religion of relatedness. We believe not only that we are all related to God by grace, but that all who are in God's covenant of grace are thereby related to one another. There is no such thing as an isolationist life of faith. Saint Paul made this clear when he wrote that the church is a body of many parts, all necessary to proper functioning. (See 1 Cor. 12:12-31.)

All Christian prayer is corporate; that is, it pertains to the whole body of believers. (*Corpus* is the Latin term for body.) Even if a Christian is alone in one room of an otherwise empty building, she or he at prayer is united to every other praying and serving Christian. C. C. Goen, late professor of church history at Wesley Seminary in Washington, D. C., loved to remind us that "although the gospel is always personal, it is never individualistic."

Ponder an interesting evidence of this: When you are in an isolated situation, how do you pray The Lord's Prayer? Do you say "My Father in heaven, ... give me today my daily bread, forgive me my sins as I forgive the sins of others, save me from the time of trial, and deliver me from evil"? Not likely. Even if you use a more traditional wording, still you most probably retain the plural pronouns—our Father, our daily bread, and so on. That is more than an incidental indication of the fact that even when we are alone we pray with the church.

For the most part it is also true that we learn to pray within the church, indeed within specific congregations. A few people who have had no exposure to Christianity may learn to pray by reading a book about prayer. But most of us have learned by attending church; as small children we overheard the congregation at prayer and came to imitate what we discovered. Even if we have come to church for the first time as adults, still it has been the whole community of faith that taught us how to pray.

Therefore personal prayer times throughout the week flow out of the congregational worship in which we participated on the previous Lord's Day and in turn flow back into the corporate worship for which we prepare on the next Lord's Day. Granted that in personal prayer at home we may confess our own sins in ways more concrete than is appropriate during a Sunday prayer of confession with the congregation; granted also that in daily prayer we may work from a longer list of concrete prayers for ourselves and others than would be appropriate on Sunday. Still, all of our personal prayers are extensions of the praying ministry of the whole church.

Even if we are hospitalized or otherwise confined so that we cannot attend the services of a congregation, still our home congregation should be a focal point of our prayer, and unless that congregation is derelict in its duty, we can be assured that its members are holding us up in prayer in the time of our confinement. Always we pray with those who are bound to us in the baptismal covenant.

In this regard we go even beyond the work of the congregation to which we belong. We pray with and for what the Nicene Creed calls the whole "catholic and apostolic church," which in our day we may more likely refer to as "the ecumenical church." Indeed, when we go into our closets and shut the door the whole company of God's people, living and dead, joins us. For those who are dead to us are yet alive to God, and in God we are one people. The venerable prayers at Holy Communion remind us that "with your people on earth and all the company of heaven" we join in praising God's name and crying: "Holy, Holy, Holy." How awesome a thought, if only we stop to ponder it!

The consciousness of this bonding of all who are in Christ should pervade and thereby alter our understanding of personal prayer, which can never be properly thought of, let alone be called, "private devotions." Always and everywhere we pray with all of God's people, united in praise and petition. This book is designed with that both as its presupposition and as its central aim for enhancing our understanding of prayer, of the church, and above all of the holy God to whom the church prays.

I. The Daily Order

Day 1

New things I now declare;
before they spring forth, I tell you of them.
Isaiah 42:9

I saw a new heaven and a new earth ...,
the new Jerusalem, coming down out of heaven from God.
Revelation 21:1-2

On the first day of each month we look ahead, recalling the many opportunities God gives us to start afresh and to begin new ventures in discipleship.

Jesus told his followers to take up the cross daily. Contrary to common belief, the cross is not some burden or challenge in life that we cannot escape and simply must endure (such as chronic disease or being unable to find work). Rather the cross is something we can evade, but we nevertheless take it up willingly, even amid misgivings. In Gethsemane Jesus reluctantly yet willingly accepted the cross that was presented to him; thus he defined his own instruction and set the pattern for discipleship.

As a new month begins, ask yourself:

Am I willing, indeed eager, to see God at work
in new ways in my life?
Will I work to identify God's newness, particularly when
it does not seem evident to me?
Am I determined to trust in God's ways,
even if I am apprehensive about what they hold in store?
Will I seek in all things to give thanks to God?

OPENING PRAYER
In the beginning, O Lord,
you created heaven and earth;
you have promised to bring forth
a new heaven and a new earth
at the end of time.
Grant therefore to all of your people
a firm conviction of your goodness and
a zeal to participate fully in whatever you intend for us,
that we may be effective witnesses to the world
in both word and deed,
a people who steadfastly proclaim your love;
through Christ our risen Savior. Amen.

CENTERING (See pages 19-21 for suggested ways of centering.)

PRAYER FOR ILLUMINATION
O Illuminator of all that exists:
As you called forth light on the first day of creation,
now by the power of your same Spirit
sweep across our emptiness and darkness,
that in reading and pondering Scripture
we may more clearly see your way
and how to walk in it boldly;
through Jesus Christ, who guides us. Amen.

PSALM 1 (Year One)
8 (Year Two)

SCRIPTURE READINGS FOR THE DAY (See pages 179-215)

CONTEMPLATION (See page 23)

ACTS APPROPRIATE TO THE DAY OF THE WEEK (See pages 103-6)

ACTS APPROPRIATE TO THE TIME OF THE YEAR (See pages 107-34)

ACTS APPROPRIATE TO THE OCCASION (See pages 135-58)

THE PRAYER OF THE WHOLE CHURCH (See pages 156-57)

CLOSING (See page 25)

Day 2

I am the LORD, that is my name;
my glory I give to no other,
nor my praise to idols.
Isaiah 42:8

I am the Alpha and the Omega,
the first and the last,
the beginning and the end.
Revelation 22:13

Consistent and conscientious discipleship springs from a sure knowl-edge that we are loved by God and that all of our devotion is a response to divine covenant love for us. Therefore, on days 2, 3, and 4 of each month we reflect on the nature of this gracious God.

The world is filled with competing deities. Even if many of the forces that allure us are not identified as gods, let alone recognized as false idols, still that is the situation. We do well, therefore, to re-examine regularly our understanding of God.

Consider how you know this God:

What passages of Scripture are for you the most powerful
   testimonies to the nature and work of God?

What long-standing convictions do Christians transmit
   to each new generation, handing on the faith of what
   the Nicene Creed calls "one holy catholic
      and apostolic church"?

What experiences can you identify in which God has been
   a crucial personal presence in your own life?

How does your understanding of God distinguish
   faith from superstition,
   deep discipleship from superficial feeling,
   and long-term promises to God from passing fancies about
      God?

OPENING PRAYER
   You alone are God. You alone are holy.
   You have made yourself known in the creation

we see all about us.
You have made yourself known in faithful covenants:
    in the journeys of Abraham and Sarah,
    in the great escape from slavery in Egypt,
    in the experiences of judges, monarchs, and mighty
        prophets.
But above all, you have revealed yourself
    in Jesus, your anointed One,
and continually you make known your presence
    in the power of the Holy Spirit,
        your sacred breath within us,
        your mighty wind around us.
You alone are God. You alone are holy. Amen.

CENTERING (See pages 19-21 for suggested ways of centering.)

PRAYER FOR ILLUMINATION
    Mighty God, our strength and hope:
    you have not left us on our own,
        struggling to find you without direction.
    Rather, you have come among us and,
        in the Scriptures of the synagogue and the church,
    you have given us the reliable record of your presence.
    Open anew the meaning of what we read,
        that by the gifts of your Holy Spirit
    we may be strengthened and sent forth
        to do your work in the world;
    through Christ who is the Living Word. Amen.

PSALM 16 (Year One)
        33:1-9 (Year Two)

SCRIPTURE READINGS FOR THE DAY (See pages 179-215)

CONTEMPLATION (See page 23)

ACTS APPROPRIATE TO THE DAY OF THE WEEK (See pages
103-6)

ACTS APPROPRIATE TO THE TIME OF THE YEAR (See pages 107-34)

ACTS APPROPRIATE TO THE OCCASION (See pages 135-58)

THE PRAYER OF THE WHOLE CHURCH (See pages 156-57)

CLOSING (See page 25)

Day 3

*The Word became flesh and lived among us, and we have seen his
glory, the glory as of a father's only son, full of grace and truth.*
John 1:14

[Christ] is the image of the invisible God....
In him all things hold together.
He is the head of the body, the church.
Colossians 1:15, 17b-18a

*In Jesus we find the clearest and most complete glimpse of the Eternal
God that we mortals are capable of experiencing.*

The church has always insisted that Jesus is far more than simply another good teacher of morals who ran afoul of conventional ideas and beliefs. Jesus is nothing less than God among us in human form. In Jesus we see the extent to which God will go to proclaim reconciliation and to demonstrate a drastic reordering of life. This is what it means to say that Christ died and arose for us.

Consider your response to God's work in Christ Jesus:

Suppose Jesus had never lived. How would your ways of
understanding God be different?

How would your motivation for doing good be different?

To what extent does gratitude for the gift of Christ
in our midst fill you with joy?

OPENING PRAYER

Jesus, Savior and Sovereign:

For our sakes, you dwelt among us in humility and patience,
that we might know more fully on earth
the ways of heaven.

Willingly you allowed yourself to be given over to death
at our hands.

Triumphantly you conquered death for us
and made us your friends
rather than the slaves of sin.

Drive from our hearts
all ingratitude,

all apathy or carelessness in following you.
Into our hearts, thus emptied,
 pour the fullness of your faithful witness,
  that the world may behold in us
   some small sign of that eternal love,
    which you have and hold within the Trinity
    and share most graciously with all who seek you. Amen.

CENTERING (See pages 19-21 for suggested ways of centering.)

PRAYER FOR ILLUMINATION
 Jesus, the world's true light:
  in your ministry on earth you read from the Scriptures
   in the synagogue
  and taught the people the meaning of what they heard.
 After your resurrection you opened the Scriptures
  to those who walked on the Emmaus road with you.
 So now, enlighten us also,
  and give us grace to do your will
  by the power of your Holy Spirit. Amen.

PSALM 23 (Year One)
  89:1-8 (Year Two)

SCRIPTURE READINGS FOR THE DAY (See pages 179-215)

CONTEMPLATION (See page 23)

ACTS APPROPRIATE TO THE DAY OF THE WEEK (See pages 103-6)

ACTS APPROPRIATE TO THE TIME OF THE YEAR (See pages 107-34)

ACTS APPROPRIATE TO THE OCCASION (See pages 135-58)

THE PRAYER OF THE WHOLE CHURCH (See pages 156-57)

CLOSING (See page 25)

Day 4

When the Advocate comes,
whom I will send to you from the Father,
the Spirit of truth who comes from the Father,
he will testify on my behalf.
John 15:26

The Spirit helps us in our weakness;
for we do not know how to pray as we ought,
but that very Spirit intercedes with sighs too deep for words.
Romans 8:26

The Holy Spirit is present and active among us.

The ascension of Jesus was not a loss, as if what he had done among us ceased. Rather it was a gain. For in the man from Nazareth, the power of God was made known for a few short years, across a limited territory. But now, by the work of the Holy Spirit, that power is let loose across the whole world for all time.

Someone has complained that for most Christians the Holy Spirit is simply "a kind of vague blur." What is your understanding of the Spirit? What works of the Spirit can you identify in your own life and in the lives of Christians across the centuries and around the world, or in your own community?

OPENING PRAYER
Come, Holy Spirit.
  You are the sacred breath, through which we have life.
  You are the blessed wind, one divine driving force
    by which we are refreshed and invigorated.
As the mists of morning that obscure the road ahead
    are dissipated before the sun's brightness,
  so clear away our confusion
    and dispel all false notions and evil intentions.
Then empower me, and all who seek your strength,
  to do your will.
Blessed are you, together with the Father and the Son,
  one God, in every age and beyond all time. Amen.

CENTERING (See pages 19-21 for suggested ways of centering.)

PRAYER FOR ILLUMINATION
  Spirit of God, unending and unfettered,
    by your divine assistance the Scriptures came into being;
    by your divine assistance their message is revealed to us.
  Therefore interpret the meaning of what we read,
      that in our day and place
  we may be refreshed and renewed
        in witness and in service to the world,
            into which you breathed life at creation itself. Amen.

PSALM 103:1-8 (Year One)
      89:11-17 (Year Two)

SCRIPTURE READINGS FOR THE DAY (See pages 179-215)

CONTEMPLATION (See page 23)

ACTS APPROPRIATE TO THE DAY OF THE WEEK (See pages 103-6)

ACTS APPROPRIATE TO THE TIME OF THE YEAR (See pages 107-34)

ACTS APPROPRIATE TO THE OCCASION (See pages 135-58)

THE PRAYER OF THE WHOLE CHURCH (See pages 156-57)

CLOSING (See page 25)

Day 5

Do not be conformed to this world,
but be transformed by
the renewing of your minds,
so that you may discern what is the will of God—
what is good and acceptable and perfect.
Romans 12:2

Be perfect ...
as your heavenly Father is perfect.
Matthew 5:48

For the past three days, our focus has been on the loving God to whom we belong. Now we consider how our love for God moves us toward transformed lives—a process sometimes referred to as "sanctification" or "going on to perfection."

To be told by Jesus that we are to be perfect as God is perfect is a terrifying thing, a command so intimidating that we snatch it from our memories—unless we think of it in terms of capacity, not identical quantity. A pint jar can be as perfectly full as a ten gallon jar, even though the amount each holds is vastly different. We are not expected to have the infinite capacity for goodness and grace that characterizes God. But we can be and are expected to live up to the human capacity God has put within each of us (in varying measures), just as the Almighty lives up to the full capacity of deity.

Further, the process of fulfilling the capacity given to us involves divine assistance. Sanctification (as this process is often called) is not a good work we do for God but a good work God does within us when we open ourselves to the One who made us, who knows our capacity, and who brings us to fulfillment when we allow it. Before this Holy One we present ourselves not as burnt offerings on an altar, but as living sacrifices in the world (Romans 12:1).

OPENING PRAYER
Accept me, O Lord, as a sacrifice,
    alive and eager to be used as you see fit.
That I am all too conformed to this world,
    I readily confess with shame.

Transform me by your mighty power.
Renew my mind,
   that I may discern your will,
   that I may both know and do
      what is good, acceptable, and perfect.
This I pray, together with the whole church;
   through that One who was
      the supremely perfect sacrifice,
   Jesus, Savior of the world. Amen.

CENTERING (See pages 19-21 for suggested ways of centering.)

PRAYER FOR ILLUMINATION
   From distraction in the midst of the sacred reading,
      save me, good Lord.
   From presuming that I already know
      the meaning of the Scriptures
         that are about to be considered, spare me.
   Pry open both my mind and my heart
         and in the place of their pretense and coldness
      put the fullness and fire of your life-giving Spirit;
   for the sake of Jesus Christ. Amen.

PSALM 17:1-8 (Year One)
         18:7-14 (Year Two)

SCRIPTURE READINGS FOR THE DAY (See pages 179-215)

CONTEMPLATION (See page 23)

ACTS APPROPRIATE TO THE DAY OF THE WEEK (See pages 103-6)

ACTS APPROPRIATE TO THE TIME OF THE YEAR (See pages 107-34)

ACTS APPROPRIATE TO THE OCCASION (See pages 135-58)

THE PRAYER OF THE WHOLE CHURCH (See pages 156-57)

CLOSING (See page 25)

Day 6

What does the LORD require of you?
To act justly
and to love mercy
and to walk humbly with your God.
Micah 6:8 NIV

Again today, we consider how our response of love for a loving God shapes our lives and propels us forward in faithful action.

The most famous words from Micah at first seem to read like a list of three things: (1) Act justly. (2) Love mercy. (3) Walk humbly with God. But it is not so.

Justice and mercy cannot be separated, at least as God defines them. Justice without mercy is harshly legalistic, even cruel. Mercy without justice sacrifices fairness on the altar of sentimentality. To the question "Is God just or is God kind?" the only proper answer is "Both." Furthermore, humility before God consists of imitating this justice-mercy of God. Humility is our response to divine love toward us and our witness to the power God's love can release in others.

Therefore what Micah sets forth is one thing, not three. We would probably be happier with three; then we could keep our little lists and check off each item in turn. But it cannot be. Hence we are constrained to ask:

If I seek justice for myself, can I understand when others
   extend mercy to those who have hurt me?
   Can I myself show mercy?
If I am merciful to others, can I understand
   why those who have been hurt
     think I have no concern for fairness?
Since God alone knows in what proportions
   justice and mercy must be mixed in any given instance,
   can I learn that walking humbly with God not only means
     that I seek to emulate God?
   It also means I cannot fully do so,
     since God alone is the righteous Judge.
How do I, with my noble aspirations, strive to emulate God
   and yet confront my limitations
     of understanding and action?
How does all of this relate to Christian teaching

about forgiving others in love,
as a loving God has forgiven us?

OPENING PRAYER
Grant to me and to all of your people, O God,
the gift of walking humbly with you.
Give us the wisdom to know how best
to temper justice with mercy,
to buttress mercy with justice,
so that your will may be done on earth as in heaven;
through Christ our Judge and Advocate. Amen.

CENTERING (See pages 19-21 for suggested ways of centering.)

PRAYER FOR ILLUMINATION
Great God, the Eternal:
By the same Holy Spirit who inspired
the writing of the Scriptures,
inspire also their reading in this hour,
that all who attentively regard these words
may know the truth and by it be set free;
through Christ who is himself
the Way, the Truth, and the Life. Amen.

PSALM 24 (Year One)
82 (Year Two)

SCRIPTURE READINGS FOR THE DAY (See pages 179-215)

CONTEMPLATION (See page 23)

ACTS APPROPRIATE TO THE DAY OF THE WEEK (See pages 103-6)

ACTS APPROPRIATE TO THE TIME OF THE YEAR (See pages 107-34)

ACTS APPROPRIATE TO THE OCCASION (See pages 135-58)

THE PRAYER OF THE WHOLE CHURCH (See pages 156-57)

CLOSING (See page 25)

Day 7

I have said these things to you
so that my joy may be in you,
and that your joy may be complete.
John 15:11

Rejoice in the Lord always;
again I will say, Rejoice.
Philippians 4:4

Our consideration of love in the preceding days began a sequence of themes set forth in Galatians 5:22 as the fruit of the Spirit: love, joy, peace, patience, kindness, generosity, faithfulness, gentleness, and self-control. Today we consider joy.

In Sunday school, children are sometimes taught this acrostic:
Jesus first.
Others next.
Yourself last.
Is this formula too childish, too simplistic to be true? Certainly it runs utterly against the grain of our culture, which advises us to "look out for Number One." (And we all know who that is.) Even in church circles we often hear this counsel given to those who spend their lives serving others in the name of Jesus: "Take time out for yourself, or you will get burned out." But what do you suppose Mother Teresa would have said had you told her that?
Wrestle valiantly with answers to these questions:
What is the source of the deepest
and most lasting joy I know?
How does this joy compare to
the fleeting frivolities that advertise themselves
as being the sources of true happiness?
In times of confusion, distress, and grief,
what does it mean to be able to
"rejoice in the Lord always"?
Consider the possibility that the best time we can take for ourselves is our time of contemplation before God, our time in conversation with God. Could it be that the lack of joy we call "burn-out" is related to our neglect of just such contemplation

and conversation with the Divine, as we seek to aid others through our own strength and wisdom alone?

OPENING PRAYER
   O God, how happy are those whose strength is in you,
   those who while going through the barren valleys of life
      make them places of springs.
   In their hearts are the highways to Zion.
   Cause us to be numbered with them,
      to find in you our dwelling place.
   Now and hereafter, grant us the delight of living in your house,
      ever singing your praise. Amen.

CENTERING (See pages 19-21 for suggested ways of centering.)

PRAYER FOR ILLUMINATION
   Author of grace and our Eternal Guide:
   As we make our pilgrimage through this life,
      shed your light upon our way, lest we slip or go astray.
   Speak to us in the recorded witness of synagogue and church
      that through the Spirit's interpretation of the Scriptures
         we may find direction and strength;
   through Christ Jesus, the Shepherd of our souls. Amen.

PSALM 4 (Year One)
         95:1-7 (Year Two)

SCRIPTURE READINGS FOR THE DAY (See pages 179-215)

CONTEMPLATION (See page 23)

ACTS APPROPRIATE TO THE DAY OF THE WEEK (See pages 103-6)

ACTS APPROPRIATE TO THE TIME OF THE YEAR (See pages 107-34)

ACTS APPROPRIATE TO THE OCCASION (See pages 135-58)

THE PRAYER OF THE WHOLE CHURCH (See pages 156-57)

CLOSING (See page 25)

Day 8

By the tender mercy of our God,
the dawn from on high will break upon us,
to give light to those who sit in darkness
and in the shadow of death,
to guide our feet into the way of peace.
Luke 1:78-79

[Christ] is our peace.
Ephesians 2:14

Today we consider peace as a fruit of the Spirit.

When the Scriptures speak of peace they intend us to understand more than the absence of enmity or hostility. The Hebrew word translated "peace" is *shalom*. *Shalom* means wholeness, the perfecting of all that is broken or incomplete. It points to reconciliation and restitution. Peace in this sense is far more than the absence of conflict or confusion. Ultimately it is the restoration of God's original intention in creation, the overcoming of sin and all resulting disruptions.

On this day it is well to ask:
How strong is my sense of having been made
whole by God?
How can I spread God's wholeness all around me?
How can I help to communicate to others
the wholeness God intends for all of us?
How can I nurture within myself the conviction
that in the end God will bring *shalom*
to the whole created order,
so that there will be "a new heaven and a new earth"?

OPENING PRAYER
Most holy and undivided Trinity:
within the complexity of your Being there is unity;
yet from that unity flows forth diversity,
and all taken together is wholeness.
Share with us this mystery of your divine life,

that we, despite our differences, may not be at odds,
    competing for power,
    struggling for prestige,
but rather may be at peace, whole as you are whole,
    conscientious trustees of your reconciling love.
Blessed are you in whose image we are made. Amen.

CENTERING (See pages 19-21 for suggested ways of centering.)

PRAYER FOR ILLUMINATION
    Come, Divine Interpreter:
    Present to us afresh the ancient words,
        lest we take them for granted as having
            small meaning for us.
    Cause your Spirit to blow around us,
        to breathe within us,
        and thus to refresh us and invigorate us
            for the work we do in your name;
    through Jesus Christ our Lord. Amen.

PSALM 131 (Year One)
        121 (Year Two)

SCRIPTURE READINGS FOR THE DAY (See pages 179-215)

CONTEMPLATION (See page 23)

ACTS APPROPRIATE TO THE DAY OF THE WEEK (See pages 103-6)

ACTS APPROPRIATE TO THE TIME OF THE YEAR (See pages 107-34)

ACTS APPROPRIATE TO THE OCCASION (See pages 135-58)

THE PRAYER OF THE WHOLE CHURCH (See pages 156-57)

CLOSING (See page 25)

Day 9

Be patient, therefore, beloved,
until the coming of the Lord.
The farmer waits for the precious crop from the earth,
being patient with it
until it receives the early and the late rains.
You also must be patient.
James 5:7-8

With the Lord one day is like a thousand years,
and a thousand years are like one day.
2 Peter 3:8

Today we consider patience as a fruit of the Spirit.

As technology presents us with newer and ever speedier "labor saving" gadgets, we become less and less practiced at patience. We wonder why it takes several seconds to place a phone call to someone half a world away, forgetting that not very long ago it took months to convey a message that distance by ship and an equal amount of time to receive a reply. Small wonder that we are strangers to the petition of the hymn writer George Croly: "Teach me the patience of unanswered prayer."

Throughout this day, take notice of your own patience or lack thereof. Ask God for greater patience, but also for the quality that underlies it: trust. Pray for trust in the graciousness of God, whose schedule may not fit our own, but whose will is always directed toward our good.

OPENING PRAYER
Eternal God:
You cannot be constrained by our ways of counting time.
Grant us, therefore, patient endurance and steadfast trust,
    so that we may wait for you without faltering and,
        as witnesses to others,
    may serve you without hesitation
        in good times or ill;
for the sake of Jesus Christ, the faithful witness. Amen.

CENTERING (See pages 19-21 for suggested ways of centering.)

PRAYER FOR ILLUMINATION
  Merciful God:
  Take from us all hardness of heart and dimness of mind.
  Remove our reluctance to know and do your will.
  Fill the church with your Spirit
    as on the Day of Pentecost,
  and open the Scriptures for the benefit of your people
    of every language, tribe, and nation;
  through Jesus, who is the Word made flesh
    in our midst.
  Amen.

PSALM 40:1-10 (Year One)
      13 (Year Two)

SCRIPTURE READINGS FOR THE DAY (See pages 179-215)

CONTEMPLATION (See page 23)

ACTS APPROPRIATE TO THE DAY OF THE WEEK (See pages 103-6)

ACTS APPROPRIATE TO THE TIME OF THE YEAR (See pages 107-34)

ACTS APPROPRIATE TO THE OCCASION (See pages 135-58)

THE PRAYER OF THE WHOLE CHURCH (See pages 156-57)

CLOSING (See page 25)

Day 10

Note then the kindness and the severity of God:
severity toward those who have fallen,
but God's kindness toward you,
provided you continue in his kindness.
Romans 11:22

Today we consider kindness as a fruit of the Spirit.

Kindness is one of those virtues we often seek to attain by deciding to do so. "I will be more kind this year" is a typical New Year's resolution. But it is broken as readily as it is made. For true kindness is a response of the heart, not a resolve of the will. It is the kindness of God toward us that engenders genuine and lasting kindness from us to others. To God's kindness we react with an enlarged spirit that makes us both more aware of the needs of others and more ready to respond as we have occasion.

While we may well examine ourselves by asking what opportunities of kindness we have missed or what occasions for kindness we might yet find, it serves us better to ask:
What kindness has God shown to me,
in forgiving my sins, in providing for my needs,
in granting me hope and everlasting life?
How can I express my gratitude for this
unmerited goodness of God?
By this means we "continue in God's kindness" as Paul puts it, rather than trying to institute our own kindness as a personal achievement to be attained by human determination.

OPENING PRAYER
Generous God,
what goodness you show to us day by day.
Your mercies never come to an end.
Like manna, they are renewed every morning.
Great is your faithfulness.
It is from you, then,
that we learn kindness and hospitality.
It is to honor and thank you

that we extend to others
the gifts you bestow upon us.
Accept what we offer as a sacrifice of praise and thanksgiving,
and grant that we may continue in your kindness forever;
through Christ, who, upon the cross, made known most fully
the extent of perfect love. Amen.

CENTERING (See pages 19-21 for suggested ways of centering.)

PRAYER FOR ILLUMINATION
Teach us, O God, by the work of your Spirit
what you are saying to us today through the sacred readings.
Thereby enable us to learn to delight in your love
and to walk in your ways;
through Jesus Christ, redeemer of the world. Amen.

PSALM 145:17-21 (Year One)
100 (Year Two)

SCRIPTURE READINGS FOR THE DAY (See pages 179-215)

CONTEMPLATION (See page 23)

ACTS APPROPRIATE TO THE DAY OF THE WEEK (See pages 103-6)

ACTS APPROPRIATE TO THE TIME OF THE YEAR (See pages 107-34)

ACTS APPROPRIATE TO THE OCCASION (See pages 135-58)

THE PRAYER OF THE WHOLE CHURCH (See pages 156-57)

CLOSING (See page 25)

Day 11

The wicked borrow, and do not pay back,
but the righteous are generous
and keep giving.
Psalm 37:21

God loves a cheerful giver.
2 Corinthians 9:7

Today we consider generosity as a fruit of the Spirit.

The gospel often sounds like sheer foolishness when judged by human wisdom. God seems not to care about how much we earn, though it is by this measure that people in our society largely judge one another. Rather God cares about how much of what we have we give away: a matter never mentioned by those who want to impress us with their incomes. Furthermore, many regard the term "cheerful giver" as an oxymoron. Surely (they suppose) it is those who cling to what they have that are "happy."

Often fund-raisers advise us to "give until it hurts." Someone, knowing that to be very bad advice, offered this alteration: "Give until it stops hurting." But even a further change is needed: "Give until it is fun, and then continue to give because it is fun." How truly happy are those who discover that it is great fun to give away money, and time and talent as well. In an ironic way, being generous may be the most self-serving style of life to be imagined. For the cheerful giver receives a joy from being generous that tightwads can never know. Such are the ways God has of surprising us.

Ask yourself this day:
    Am I a cheerful giver or a reluctant one?
    When giving something away,
        do I ever quietly utter this prayer:
      "O Lord, help me to give away even more"?
    How often do I recall John Wesley's rule:
      "Earn all you can. Save all you can. Give away all you can"?
    How can I increase both my gifts
    and my eagerness to give?

OPENING PRAYER
God of high heaven:
By coming to earth to dwell among us,
    to die for us,
you have demonstrated the greatest generosity possible.
Enable us to see in the manger and the cross
    the joy of giving ourselves fully in your service.
Snatch from us the fear that if we give away what we have,
    we will have less—or even nothing.
Cause us to know that those who would save their lives,
    lose them,
    while those who lose their lives
        for the sake of the gospel truly find them.
We pray through him who taught us this
    in both word and deed,
    Jesus Christ, the perfect offering. Amen.

CENTERING (See pages 19-21 for suggested ways of centering.)

PRAYER FOR ILLUMINATION
God, our guide and helper:
In the Scriptures you have given us the resources
    to find the way of life you intend for us.
Now, by your Spirit's faithfulness,
    enable us to understand this way without distortion
    and to walk in it without timidity;
through Jesus Christ our Savior. Amen.

PSALM 37:21-26 (Year One)
        112:1-7 (Year Two)

SCRIPTURE READINGS FOR THE DAY (See pages 179-215)

CONTEMPLATION (See page 23)

ACTS APPROPRIATE TO THE DAY OF THE WEEK (See pages 103-6)

ACTS APPROPRIATE TO THE TIME OF THE YEAR (See pages 107-34)

ACTS APPROPRIATE TO THE OCCASION (See pages 135-58)

THE PRAYER OF THE WHOLE CHURCH (See pages 156-57)

CLOSING (See page 25)

Day 12

Be strong in the grace that is in Christ Jesus;
and what you have heard from me
through many witnesses
entrust to faithful people
who will be able to teach others as well.
2 Timothy 2:1-2

Today we consider faithfulness as a fruit of the Spirit.

Faithfulness begins with God. Why would we want to commit ourselves to an untrustworthy deity? It is the reliability *of* God that is the basis for our faithfulness *to* God. The Scriptures place great stress on the dependability of God, precisely so that we can join confidently in the covenant God opens to us. Once we have done this, we are called to be a faithful people.

But there is yet one more step in the process. The faithful people of God are to "teach others as well." That is, we are to be witnesses to the reliability of God so that those who have not committed themselves to covenant faithfulness may come to believe. If we are not faithful, we place in their way a stumbling block over which they may fall.

On this day, then, we pray for grace to trust in God's goodness, to keep our vows with fidelity, and to be those who instruct others in the way.

OPENING PRAYER
    God of all ages:
    In every time and place you have been steadfast.
    Your faithfulness endures without fail
        from generation to generation.
    So bind to yourself the hearts of your covenant people
        that all who have promised fidelity to the gospel
        may fulfill their vows.
    Preserve your church
        not only from renunciation or neglect of faith
        but also from a tepid faith that calls forth from others
        contempt rather than conversion.

Make your church to be as a city set upon a hill,
    that our witness may be seen
    and that others may be drawn to you.
For the sake of Jesus Christ, who is faithful in all things. Amen.

CENTERING (See pages 19-21 for suggested ways of centering.)

PRAYER FOR ILLUMINATION
    You, O God, gave ancient writers the grace to record
        their experiences of your work in their midst.
    So give us also the grace to discover your hand in our day,
        as the Scriptures are read and pondered.
    Illumine us with the Spirit's brightness
        that we may see clearly your truth and will for us;
    through the merits and mediation of Christ our Lord. Amen.

PSALM 31:19-24 (Year One)
    32 (Year Two)

SCRIPTURE READINGS FOR THE DAY (See pages 179-215)

CONTEMPLATION (See page 23)

ACTS APPROPRIATE TO THE DAY OF THE WEEK (See pages 103-6)

ACTS APPROPRIATE TO THE TIME OF THE YEAR (See pages 107-34)

ACTS APPROPRIATE TO THE OCCASION (See pages 135-58)

THE PRAYER OF THE WHOLE CHURCH (See pages 156-57)

CLOSING (See page 25)

Day 13

The Lord's servant must not be quarrelsome
but kindly to everyone,
an apt teacher,
patient,
correcting opponents with gentleness.
2 Timothy 2:24-25

Today we consider gentleness as a fruit of the Spirit.

From birth onward, we seem to know instinctively how to be harsh and even cruel, particularly to those with whom we disagree. Most of us have mastered well the skills of sarcasm and superiority. Gentleness, on the other hand, seems to be something we have to learn, particularly when dealing with those who strongly oppose us.

Yet who among us would not prefer that we ourselves be corrected by a gentle person rather than by someone whose manner is rude and caustic? Paul asks the Corinthians a question whose answer is a foregone conclusion: "What would you prefer? Am I to come to you with a stick, or with love in a spirit of gentleness?"

In our interactions at home, at church, in the workplace, in the world at large, the gentle manner of a Christian believer is a powerful testimony to the alluring gentleness of the Christ to whom we are to bear witness.

OPENING PRAYER
Give grace, O Lord Jesus, as I seek your way,
    that I may grow more and more into your likeness
    and that I may bear your ensign
        as a banner of hope and direction
        before all who are distraught or confused.
Through this time of daily devotion
    instill in me your own gentleness,
    quiet my over-wrought alarms,
    and enable me to rest confidently in your wisdom.
These things grant by the power of your Holy Spirit. Amen.

CENTERING (See pages 19-21 for suggested ways of centering.)

PRAYER FOR ILLUMINATION
    Eternal and expansive One:
    you have willingly come to me in the confines of my little world
        to stretch me,
        to open before me unimagined paths.
    Through the reading and study of the Scriptures,
        continue to work in and through me,
        that by the power of your Holy Spirit
           I may more fully become
             what you intend for me to be.
    Through Christ the Redeemer. Amen.

PSALM 15 (Year One)
        139:1-12 (Year Two)

SCRIPTURE READINGS FOR THE DAY (See pages 179-215)

CONTEMPLATION (See page 23)

ACTS APPROPRIATE TO THE DAY OF THE WEEK (See pages 103-6)

ACTS APPROPRIATE TO THE TIME OF THE YEAR (See pages 107-34)

ACTS APPROPRIATE TO THE OCCASION (See pages 135-58)

THE PRAYER OF THE WHOLE CHURCH (See pages 156-57)

CLOSING (See page 25)

Day 14

Like a city breached, without walls,
is one who lacks self-control.
Proverbs 25:28

Athletes exercise self-control in all things;
they do it to receive a perishable wreath,
but we an imperishable one.
1 Corinthians 9:25

Today we consider self-control as a fruit of the Spirit.

Self-discipline is not a favorite pursuit for most of us. Self-indulgence is the more popular pursuit, for that is much less work and certainly more fun—in the short term. In the verse above from 1 Corinthians, Paul seeks to motivate us by comparing the short and the long view of things. The wreaths of wilting laurel leaves placed upon the heads of winning athletes in ancient times is not to be compared to what James 1:12 calls "the crown of life that the Lord has promised to those who love him."

As a part of your offering to God today, honestly answer these questions:

In what parts of my life do I have sufficient self-control?
In what areas do I need to improve?
Am I determined to bring about improvement
with the help of God?

OPENING PRAYER
God, you call me to ever greater devotion and service.
Help me to have under control
every impulse that distracts me from loving you,
every impediment that disrupts my work for you.
As a trainer prepares an athlete for the contest, so discipline me
that I may grow in strength and endurance
and may receive the crown of life from your hand.
Shine forth with such beauty
that I may willingly accept even
your necessary correction of me,

that I may value above all your eternal realm
and its righteousness;
through Jesus Christ, the pioneer and perfecter of our faith.
Amen.

CENTERING (See pages 19-21 for suggested ways of centering.)

PRAYER FOR ILLUMINATION
Without your aid, O God,
I cannot begin to understand you.
But because you would not have yourself to be unknown,
you have given us a record of your work
from creation onward,
set down for us by
poets, prophets, apostles, and evangelists.
Through this record read and pondered,
give to me what I need
and strengthen me to accomplish your purposes for me.
Grant this, holy and undivided Trinity,
for the honor of your name. Amen.

PSALM 141:1-8 (Year One)
119:101-108 (Year Two)

SCRIPTURE READINGS FOR THE DAY (See pages 179-215)

CONTEMPLATION (See page 23)

ACTS APPROPRIATE TO THE DAY OF THE WEEK (See pages 103-6)

ACTS APPROPRIATE TO THE TIME OF THE YEAR (See pages 107-34)

ACTS APPROPRIATE TO THE OCCASION (See pages 135-58)

THE PRAYER OF THE WHOLE CHURCH (See pages 156-57)

CLOSING (See page 25)

Day 15

Search me, O God, and know my heart;
test me and know my thoughts.
See if there is any wicked way in me,
and lead me in the way everlasting.
Psalm 139:23-24

I am the one who searches minds and hearts.
Revelation 2:23

At the midpoint of each month, we have finished our consideration of the fruits of the Spirit. Before proceeding to a consideration of the Beatitudes, we pause for a time of reflection and self-examination.

Ask yourself these questions. When an honest answer is not to your liking, ask God for the strength and wisdom to improve.

What have I done in the past two weeks to help others:
to console the distraught, to assist the weak,
to guide the confused, and so on?
What have I done to alleviate the larger causes of
human suffering:
to seek justice, to advance the humane treatment of all,
to overcome the oppression and exploitation of the weak,
to speak up in the defense of those
who were misrepresented or mistreated?
Have I participated in the weekly worship of the congregation?
Have I received the Supper of the Lord?
If so, has it been for me since then a sign of the presence
and power of the risen Lord in our midst?
How faithful have I been in daily devotions,
and what benefit have I received from these
that has strengthened me for service to others?
In these devotions, have I remembered those for whom
prayers were asked in congregational worship?
Does fasting or abstinence in an appropriate form
commend itself to me today?

OPENING PRAYER
  Maker and ruler of all:
  Govern my life by your wisdom and counsel.
  Forgive me in those areas where I have failed you,
    and strengthen me further wherein I have served you well.
  Save me from complacency
    and smugness over my spiritual successes
  as much as from despair
    and guilt over my spiritual failures.
  Grant in increasing measure the gift of your Holy Spirit to me,
      that I may grow in grace
        and thus more fully praise you day by day;
    through Christ who strengthens me. Amen.

CENTERING (See pages 19-21 for suggested ways of centering.)

PRAYER FOR ILLUMINATION
  The eyes of my heart, O God,
    are clouded over by daily cares and fears.
  By the power of your Holy Spirit,
    restore my sight.
  Cause the scales to fall from my eyes
    through the study of your holy Scriptures,
      that I may suffer no confusion
        but walk forth in confidence,
    with your Word being a lamp to my feet
      and a light to my pathway;
  through Christ who is true light and vision. Amen.

PSALM 27:1-8 (Year One)
      27:11-14 (Year Two)

SCRIPTURE READINGS FOR THE DAY (See pages 179-215)

CONTEMPLATION (See page 23)

ACTS APPROPRIATE TO THE DAY OF THE WEEK (See pages 103-6)

ACTS APPROPRIATE TO THE TIME OF THE YEAR (See pages 107-34)

ACTS APPROPRIATE TO THE OCCASION (See pages 135-58)

THE PRAYER OF THE WHOLE CHURCH (See pages 156-57)

CLOSING (See page 25)

Day 16

This poor soul cried, and was heard by the LORD,
and was saved from every trouble.
Psalm 34:6

If you close your ear to the cry of the poor,
you will cry out and not be heard.
Proverbs 21:13

Today we begin a consideration of the Beatitudes. The translation used each day is that of The Jerusalem Bible.

Beatitude 1: How happy are the poor in spirit;
theirs is the kingdom of heaven.

We are most accustomed to Matthew's version of the first beatitude, quoted above. Luke says simply, "How happy are the poor." So who are meant: those who literally have no possessions, or those who, having many possessions, nevertheless know the limits of these and therefore seek spiritual riches?

Is it necessary to exclude one of these options? Do not both the literal poor and those affluent persons who admit to their spiritual poverty have the same sense of dependency—and of gratitude when their cry for help is heard? Further, both make legitimate claims upon those who are in a position to assist them. We are commanded to alleviate the suffering of the financially poor as we ourselves have ability; we are also called to assist the poor in spirit by sharing with them whatever spiritual resources we ourselves have been given. The kingdom of heaven consists of mutuality as well as of grace.

OPENING PRAYER
God of the poor,
from the riches of your grace
you share your bounty with all who are in need.
Provide for the hungry and the homeless,
and teach us to do likewise,
so that none may be prevented by physical circumstances

from loving and serving you with joy and strength.
So also provide for all whose spirits suffer poverty,
that none may doubt your goodness
or overlook your faithfulness.
Above all, prevent us from thinking we are rich in spirit—
if instead we are wretched, pitiable, poor, blind, and naked
—lest our self-deception separate us from you.
This we ask through our Lord Jesus Christ
who, though he was rich, for our sakes became poor,
so that, by his poverty, we might become rich. Amen.

CENTERING (See pages 19-21 for suggested ways of centering.)

PRAYER FOR ILLUMINATION
By the generosity of your heart, O God,
you have given us abundant evidence of your love.
As the Scriptures are read and pondered
teach us that we dare not rely on our own understanding
but only on that understanding
which you have so freely offered
through Christ our teacher and redeemer. Amen.

PSALM 119:1-8 (Year One)
41 (Year Two)

SCRIPTURE READINGS FOR THE DAY (See pages 179-215)

CONTEMPLATION (See page 23)

ACTS APPROPRIATE TO THE DAY OF THE WEEK (See pages 103-6)

ACTS APPROPRIATE TO THE TIME OF THE YEAR (See pages 107-34)

ACTS APPROPRIATE TO THE OCCASION (See pages 135-58)

THE PRAYER OF THE WHOLE CHURCH (See pages 156-57)

CLOSING (See page 25)

Day 17

After you have suffered for a little while, the God of all grace,
who has called you to his eternal glory in Christ,
will himself restore, support, strengthen, and establish you.
1 Peter 5:10

The spirit of the Lord GOD is upon me . . .
to comfort all who mourn,
to provide for those who mourn in Zion—
to give them a garland instead of ashes,
the oil of gladness instead of mourning,
the mantle of praise instead of a faint spirit.
Isaiah 61:1-3

> *Beatitude 2: Happy those who mourn:*
> *they shall be comforted.*

As with yesterday's beatitude, there can be two meanings, and we need not exclude either. There are those who literally mourn; for them the promise of the resurrection is the greatest source of strength—for "comfort" means "to make strong." But there are those who mourn figuratively, those who regret their sins and grieve over their errors. God strengthens them also, by the assurance of forgiveness. It is those who refuse to mourn their sins about whom God can do little. But those who do mourn and turn to God are strengthened.

OPENING PRAYER
  O God,
    you are a strong tower and a sure defense
        in the time of trouble.
  Without you, we have no certain help.
  But always you come to us, pointing us
        to Mount Calvary
        and to an empty tomb beyond it.
  You are our gain in the time of loss,
  our forgiveness and direction
    after we have erred and strayed like lost sheep.

To you be praise and glory
  through Christ, who strengthens us to do all things. Amen.

CENTERING (See pages 19-21 for suggested ways of centering.)

PRAYER FOR ILLUMINATION
  We await the strengthening power of your Word,
    O God of hope.
  Help us so
    to remember your wonders of old,
    to meditate on all of your work
        both day and night,
  that we may be like trees planted by streams of water,
    which yield their fruit in its season.
  By the goodness of your Spirit,
    make us fruitful branches
        as we ponder what you say to us now;
  through Christ, the true vine and tree of life. Amen.

PSALM 34:15-22 (Year One)
        43 (Year Two)

SCRIPTURE READINGS FOR THE DAY (See pages 179-215)

CONTEMPLATION (See page 23)

ACTS APPROPRIATE TO THE DAY OF THE WEEK (See pages 103-6)

ACTS APPROPRIATE TO THE TIME OF THE YEAR (See pages 107-34)

ACTS APPROPRIATE TO THE OCCASION (See pages 135-58)

THE PRAYER OF THE WHOLE CHURCH (See pages 156-57)

CLOSING (See page 25)

Day 18

Concerning God's chosen one:
He shall not judge by what his eyes see,
or decide by what his ears hear;
but with righteousness he shall judge the poor,
and decide with equity for the meek of the earth.
Isaiah 11:3-4

The meek shall inherit the land,
and delight themselves in abundant prosperity.
Psalm 37:11

> *Beatitude 3: Happy the gentle:*
> *they shall have the earth for their heritage.*

Meekness has gotten a bad name in our day. We think the meek are those who allow themselves to be used as doormats; so "meekness" and "weakness" have become synonyms. But the translation of the third beatitude as given above uses instead the term "the gentle." We considered gentleness as a fruit of the Spirit on Day 13, and that is a key for our understanding of this and indeed of all of the Beatitudes.

The meek inherit; they do not earn. The earth is promised to them as their heritage, not their wages. The attributes commended to us are gifts from God, from a God who does not judge by what the eyes see or the ears hear. Thus this God turns upside down our usual values. Note well that in the Beatitudes happiness is not promised to the wealthy, the powerful, the glamorous, or those with sex appeal. In that reversal of our usual expectations, we find God's gift to us, as strange as it may seem.

How should this biblical approach to what is important change your own values, your own estimate of what constitutes "success"? By the way, how successful do you suppose Jesus was considered to be on the day he died on the cross?

OPENING PRAYER
God, your thoughts are not our thoughts,
and your ways are not our ways.
We confess our bewilderment at learning
of the strange values you treasure.

Transform us so drastically that we may embrace
  your ways without fear or embarrassment.
Enable us to judge beyond
    what human eyes can see or ears can hear,
  that you may regard us as the meek,
    worthy inheritors of your mercy;
through Jesus Christ, in whom is true happiness. Amen.

CENTERING (See pages 19-21 for suggested ways of centering.)

PRAYER FOR ILLUMINATION
  O God,
    as the Scriptures are opened before us,
   by the grace of the Holy Spirit
   take away the dullness of our hearts.
  Let no preoccupation with other matters distract us
    from heeding your message,
    from doing your work in our day and place.
  For making known your ways to us,
    we bless you, Holy Trinity, now and forever. Amen.

PSALM 25:4-15 (Year One)
      37:1-11 (Year Two)

SCRIPTURE READINGS FOR THE DAY (See pages 179-215)

CONTEMPLATION (See page 23)

ACTS APPROPRIATE TO THE DAY OF THE WEEK (See pages 103-6)

ACTS APPROPRIATE TO THE TIME OF THE YEAR (See pages 107-34)

ACTS APPROPRIATE TO THE OCCASION (See pages 135-58)

THE PRAYER OF THE WHOLE CHURCH (See pages 156-57)

CLOSING (See page 25)

Day 19

Here is what the Lord says to you:
How long will you judge unjustly
and show partiality to the wicked?
Give justice to the weak and the orphan;
maintain the right of the lowly and the destitute.
Psalm 82:2-3

Whatever is true, whatever is honorable,
whatever is just, whatever is pure,
whatever is pleasing, whatever is commendable ...
think about these things.
Philippians 4:8

> *Beatitude 4: Happy those who hunger and thirst for what is right:*
> *they shall be satisfied.*

To be famished for that which is right and just and honest: That is an assignment God gives each of us at baptism, and God calls us to spend all the rest of our lives working earnestly on that task.

When you hear of corruption in public life, are you simply so disgusted that you want to become disengaged from the whole political process? Or do you so greatly hunger and thirst for what is right that you are willing to get out of your easy chair and do something to demand integrity? When close friends or family members act unjustly (or simply condone injustice in conversation), are you so starved for what is right that you take time to help them onto a better path—perhaps risking their rejection in the process?

For those of us who do not like to "rock the boat," these are not easy questions. But "hungering and thirsting" in this beatitude does not refer to wanting a snack between meals, but to being starved for what is right.

OPENING PRAYER
To all of your people, O Lord,
give such a longing for what is right
that none of us can tolerate the wrong

for one more day.
What we must do to set things right, enable us to do
    with firmness and fairness,
        without self-righteousness
        or a pretended wisdom.
And give us grace to submit to your correction
        when we are unjust,
lest the good things for which we stand be sullied
        by our own wrongdoing or inaction.
This we pray through him whose ideals and deeds
        were never at odds,
Christ our Savior. Amen.

CENTERING (See pages 19-21 for suggested ways of centering.)

PRAYER FOR ILLUMINATION
    God ever good:
    as we open before you the pages of Scripture,
    open to us
        the bread of life,
        the cup of salvation,
    that we, who hunger and thirst for your word,
        may be satisfied and
        may share with others
    what you have shared with us to overflowing;
    through the One who is both provider and judge. Amen.

PSALM 11 (Year One)
        143:1-8 (Year Two)

SCRIPTURE READINGS FOR THE DAY (See pages 179-215)

CONTEMPLATION (See page 23)

ACTS APPROPRIATE TO THE DAY OF THE WEEK (See pages
103-6)

ACTS APPROPRIATE TO THE TIME OF THE YEAR (See pages
107-34)

ACTS APPROPRIATE TO THE OCCASION (See pages 135-58)

THE PRAYER OF THE WHOLE CHURCH (See pages 156-57)

CLOSING (See page 25)

Day 20

Love your enemies, do good, and lend,
expecting nothing in return....
Be merciful,
just as your Father is merciful.
Luke 6:35-36

> *Beatitude 5: Happy the merciful:*
> *they shall have mercy shown them.*

There is an engaging reciprocity about the gospel. Because God is merciful to us, we are to be merciful to others—even to our enemies—without expecting anything in return. Yet the fifth beatitude suggests that those who are merciful will in return receive yet more mercy.

Is this a tit-for-tat business arrangement in which God forgives us only as much as we forgive others? Or is it like opening a rolled-up plastic bag: The more we open it, the more we can put into it; and the more we put into it, the more open it becomes. It is not a matter of tit for tat but rather of making increasingly available a capacity already there in potential.

Ponder the potential for mercy God has given you:

To what extent have you used it?

How might you use it more effectively?

To whom do you need to show mercy as a gift
so that they may understand more fully
God's gracious gift of forgiveness?

OPENING PRAYER

God of all mercies:
To us you extend forgiveness and help again and again.
Spare us from supposing either
that your mercy is automatic,
or that we must earn or deserve it.
Confront us with the mystery of your grace,
which is beyond all human comprehension.
Cause us to be merciful in your name,
that those who see us

may see beyond us
and find you there.
Through Christ, your mercy made flesh. Amen.

CENTERING (See pages 19-21 for suggested ways of centering.)

PRAYER FOR ILLUMINATION
O God,
out of your loving kindness you have given us the Scriptures,
that in their testimony we may discover your way.
By the power of your Holy Spirit
overcome all obstacles we put in front of you,
as we seek to protect ourselves
from a divine goodness we find uncomfortable.
Remove from us all sense of threat,
and in its place put love.
For your perfect love casts out all fear;
through Jesus Christ our Lord. Amen.

PSALM 130 (Year One)
145:1-9 (Year Two)

SCRIPTURE READINGS FOR THE DAY (See pages 179-215)

CONTEMPLATION (See page 23)

ACTS APPROPRIATE TO THE DAY OF THE WEEK (See pages 103-6)

ACTS APPROPRIATE TO THE TIME OF THE YEAR (See pages 107-34)

ACTS APPROPRIATE TO THE OCCASION (See pages 135-58)

THE PRAYER OF THE WHOLE CHURCH (See pages 156-57)

CLOSING (See page 25)

Day 21

I do not understand my own actions.
For I do not do what I want,
but I do the very thing I hate.
Romans 7:15

Teach me your way, O LORD,
that I may walk in your truth;
give me an undivided heart to revere your name.
Psalm 86:11

> *Beatitude 6: Happy the pure in heart:*
> *they shall see God.*

The nineteenth-century lay theologian Søren Kierkegaard wrote that "purity of heart is to will one thing." One thing, not two—between which we must then choose. But how to achieve such unity of purpose? How often have you said about some spiritual challenge: "On the one hand, I want to go in this direction, but on the other hand I am drawn to the opposite way"?

Even Paul the apostle confessed that too often he wanted to do one thing yet did another. Ultimately Paul resolved his conflict by seeing that in his own power he could not be always of one mind; only Christ could deliver him from his spiritual confusion. (See Romans 7:21-25.)

Could it be that this beatitude is not saying that first we must have purity of desire and as a reward will see God? Could it be instead that when we pray to be delivered from a double mind we see God in ways that only God can know? How appropriate to keep offering the petition of the psalmist quoted above, to seek an undivided heart.

OPENING PRAYER
　Majestic God, glowing in a splendor I cannot bear to see:
　　Show me as much of yourself as I have eyes to behold.
　　For the rest, let me simply entrust myself to your goodness.
　Remove from me selfish motives
　　and those evil intentions that I have mingled

with holy desires.
Create in me a clean heart, O God,
  and put a new and right spirit within me.
For you only can do this;
through Jesus Christ, who in Gethsemane faced down
  the demons that divide us. Amen.

CENTERING (See pages 19-21 for suggested ways of centering.)

PRAYER FOR ILLUMINATION
  Let the words of my mouth
    and the meditation of my heart
    be acceptable to you, O Lord,
  that what I read and consider within
    may transform me outwardly;
  through Christ, my rock and my redeemer. Amen.

PSALM 51:1-12 (Year One)
      86:8-15 (Year Two)

SCRIPTURE READINGS FOR THE DAY (See pages 179-215)

CONTEMPLATION (See page 23)

ACTS APPROPRIATE TO THE DAY OF THE WEEK (See pages 103-6)

ACTS APPROPRIATE TO THE TIME OF THE YEAR (See pages 107-34)

ACTS APPROPRIATE TO THE OCCASION (See pages 135-58)

THE PRAYER OF THE WHOLE CHURCH (See pages 156-57)

CLOSING (See page 25)

Day 22

In Christ God was reconciling the world to himself,
not counting their trespasses against them,
and entrusting the message of reconciliation to us.
So we are ambassadors for Christ,
since God is making his appeal through us.
2 Corinthians 5:19-20

Be at peace among yourselves.
1 Thessalonians 5:13

> *Beatitude 7: Happy the peacemakers:*
> *they shall be called sons [and daughters] of God.*

One of the world's most coveted honors is the Nobel Peace Prize, and one of the world's most popular prayers begins, "Lord, make me an instrument of your peace." How ironic, then, that we seldom think it is our calling to be peacemakers! On Day 8, we looked at the nature of peace. But today we look at the mission given to us to bring about reconciliation wherever we encounter alienation from God or discord between humans.

Do we too often assume that our assignment is to "stay out of it" when we encounter strained relationships? Sometimes that may be true—except that always we are to pray for reconciliation, and always we are to avoid any action that exacerbates the problem: particularly the carrying of tales from one side of the conflict to the other and participation in gossipy misrepresentation and exaggeration, both of which fuel the fires of animosity.

But peacemaking is more than passivity. God actively engaged in peacemaking in the Incarnation; so surely those who are to be known as daughters and sons of this God are called to be active in passing the peace. That latter phrase may be a helpful clue. Most congregations these days have a segment in the worship service called "the passing of the peace." Too often it is perfunctory, merely an exercise in polite civility, detached from any concrete action in daily life. So here is a suggestion that may make it more meaningful and at the same time may make you more aware of your calling to be an ambassador for Christ. Every time you exchange the peace with others in a worship service, quietly say to yourself: "God calls me to be a peacemaker at every opportunity available to me."

OPENING PRAYER
O God, author of peace and its most active proponent:
so greatly did you desire the reconciliation
of all things to you
that in Christ you assumed the humility
of an earthly existence,
indeed the humiliation of death by public execution.
Give me grace to risk comfort and status
in order that others may be at peace with you
and with one another.
In this cause, strengthen me through
this time of devotion today;
through Christ who offers perfect peace to all. Amen.

CENTERING (See pages 18-20 for suggested ways of centering.)

PRAYER FOR ILLUMINATION
By your tender mercies, O God,
by the unceasing ministry of your Spirit,
open the meaning of the ancient documents
handed on by communities of believers,
so that in this time and place
I may better understand how I may best work
to heal your fractured world;
in Jesus' name. Amen.

PSALM 33 (Year One)
        122 (Year Two)

SCRIPTURE READINGS FOR THE DAY (See pages 179-215)

CONTEMPLATION (See page 23)

ACTS APPROPRIATE TO THE DAY OF THE WEEK (See pages 103-6)

ACTS APPROPRIATE TO THE TIME OF THE YEAR (See pages 107-34)

ACTS APPROPRIATE TO THE OCCASION (See pages 135-58)

THE PRAYER OF THE WHOLE CHURCH (See pages 156-57)

CLOSING (See page 25)

Day 23

Live your life in a manner worthy of the gospel of Christ....
For [God] has graciously granted you the privilege ...
of suffering for him....
Do nothing from selfish ambition or conceit,
but in humility regard others as better than yourselves.
Let each of you look not to your own interests,
but to the interests of others.
Philippians 1:27, 29; 2:3-4

Beatitude 8: Happy those who are persecuted in the cause of right:
theirs is the kingdom of heaven.

Any dummy can be obnoxious enough to elicit persecution. It takes neither talent nor concentration. But to call forth persecution *in the cause of right*, that is quite another matter. Our capacity for self-deception is enormous. Thus we can convince ourselves we are both working for the right cause and working at it in the right way, when in truth we are engaging in self-serving actions that detract from the causes we think we promote. It is possible to stand in the way of what is right, even when we are intending to walk in right paths. Therefore our urgent need is to see ourselves as our critics see us.

When we are derided for the causes we espouse, it is well to ask:
Is the object of derision the cause I support
   or my imperfect way of expressing that cause?
When I feel constrained to criticize others,
   am I criticizing their causes and viewpoints
      or them personally?
Do I feel a sense of deep sadness within
   when I must stand against others,
or do I feel a secret sense of glee or of superiority?
Do I want to see those who criticize me
   persuaded and transformed
   or defeated and punished?
How can I better be faithful to what I believe
   and at the same time

be tender and compassionate in my manner,
and open to new understandings within myself?

In the kingdom of heaven the impurities of wrong motives for
right actions cannot exist. They are refined away by the fire of
divine goodness.

OPENING PRAYER
Remember, O Lord, all who are unjustly accused
or wrongfully treated
because they stand for what is right.
To such persons give the comfort of your presence now
and the assurance that they shall share
in your triumph over all evil
at the coming of your Kingdom.
Grant us also to stand for what is right,
and to do this always with pure intention and wise action,
that the causes we support
may commend themselves
to the world
without distractions we create;
through Jesus who, without thought for himself,
called forth the ultimate persecution
and achieved the final victory. Amen.

CENTERING (See pages 19-21 for suggested ways of centering.)

PRAYER FOR ILLUMINATION
Open to me now, O Lord,
the mysteries of your grace,
to the extent that I can know them,
and for all else, enable me simply
to trust your goodness. Amen.

PSALM 3 (Year One)
9:1-14 (Year Two)

SCRIPTURE READINGS FOR THE DAY (See pages 179-215)

CONTEMPLATION (See page 23)

ACTS APPROPRIATE TO THE DAY OF THE WEEK (See pages 103-6)

ACTS APPROPRIATE TO THE TIME OF THE YEAR (See pages 107-34)

ACTS APPROPRIATE TO THE OCCASION (See pages 135-58)

THE PRAYER OF THE WHOLE CHURCH (See pages 156-57)

CLOSING (See page 25)

Day 24

If one member suffers, all suffer together with it;
if one member is honored, all rejoice together with it.
Now you are the body of Christ
and individually members of it.
1 Corinthians 12:26-27

Let us consider how we may spur one another on
toward love and good deeds.
Let us not give up meeting together,
as some are in the habit of doing,
but let us encourage one another.
Hebrews 10:24-25 NIV

Today's theme is life in community.

As it takes an entire village to raise a child, so also it takes an entire congregation to nurture a Christian. God has created human beings in an interlocking system of relationships, apart from which we cannot flourish. The church is a gift from God in order that we may be provided with a community of faith in which to grow; in the process this community holds us accountable and encourages us in our spiritual journey. Regular participation in the life of a congregation is intended to be mutually beneficial. As others spur us on, so we also spur others on.

We are initiated into this community at baptism. Even death does not separate us from it but rather translates us into another form of it, so that Charles Wesley could write: "One family we dwell in God, one church above, beneath, though now divided by the stream, the narrow stream of death."

What do you cherish most about your life in a Christian congregation? What do you think are your major contributions to others in the congregation?

OPENING PRAYER
O God of hosts: You are never alone.
Even when you seem to us to be solitary in your splendor,
you yourself live within the community

80

of your triune being.
As you are never alone,
    so you provide that we shall not be alone.
Increase our appreciation for your gift of the church,
    imperfect though it is because of our many faults.
By the unifying power of the Holy Spirit,
    visit us and bind us together as those
who know themselves to be your people;
through Jesus Christ, whose promises we trust. Amen.

CENTERING (See pages 19-21 for suggested ways of centering.)

PRAYER FOR ILLUMINATION
    Thanks be to you, O God, for synagogue and church,
        communities of people that have preserved for us
        the written testimonies of their experience with you.
    By the same Spirit that worked among them
        minister to us
    that what we read and ponder
        may enliven us and stretch us;
    through Christ our Savior. Amen.

PSALM 115:1-8 (Year One)
        115:9-18 (Year Two)

SCRIPTURE READINGS FOR THE DAY (See pages 179-215)

CONTEMPLATION (See page 23)

ACTS APPROPRIATE TO THE DAY OF THE WEEK (See pages 103-6)

ACTS APPROPRIATE TO THE TIME OF THE YEAR (See pages 107-34)

ACTS APPROPRIATE TO THE OCCASION (See pages 135-58)

THE PRAYER OF THE WHOLE CHURCH (See pages 156-57)

CLOSING (See page 25)

Day 25

I ask not only on behalf of these,
but also on behalf of those who will believe in me through their word,
that they may all be one ...
that they may become completely one,
so that the world may know that you have sent me.
John 17:20-21, 23

There is one body and one Spirit,
just as you were called to the one hope of your calling,
one Lord, one faith, one baptism,
one God and Father of all,
who is above all and through all and in all.
Ephesians 4:4-6

For the next four days, we consider in turn four characteristics of the church set forth in the Nicene Creed: "We believe in the one holy catholic and apostolic church." Today we pray for the unity of Christ's church.

In the face of the practical realities that the world can plainly see, it seems absurd to affirm that the church is "one." The body of Christ on earth suffers more divisions than we can count. Just when it seems that one fracture has been mended, another erupts. Taken together, our disagreements cause the world confusion at best, and at worst scorn mixed with laughter.

Therefore prayer for the unity of the church is an urgent task for all Christians. And in our praying, surely we must ask:

What have we and the congregations of our heritage contributed to the disruption of unity?

What have we contributed to mutual understanding and progress toward unity?

OPENING PRAYER
As you are one, O God,
make the people of your new covenant one.
Help us to distinguish between
what you deem to be essential
and what we find to be merely convenient and comfortable.

Strengthen us for the hard work of overcoming differences
  we have wrongly held and cherished for generations,
  disagreements that undermine our efforts
    to share the gospel message of reconciliation.
Bind up the wounds of your church and make it truly one body,
  through Christ who is its head. Amen.

CENTERING (See pages 19-21 for suggested ways of centering.)

PRAYER FOR ILLUMINATION
  God of light and love:
  Send forth your Spirit to remove all obstacles
    to the understanding and doing of your Word,
  so that your goodness may be proclaimed
    by those who follow you
  as disciples of Christ Jesus. Amen.

PSALM 99 (Year One)
       133 (Year Two)

SCRIPTURE READINGS FOR THE DAY (See pages 179-215)

CONTEMPLATION (See page 23)

ACTS APPROPRIATE TO THE DAY OF THE WEEK (See pages 103-6)

ACTS APPROPRIATE TO THE TIME OF THE YEAR (See pages 107-34)

ACTS APPROPRIATE TO THE OCCASION (See pages 135-58)

THE PRAYER OF THE WHOLE CHURCH (See pages 156-57)

CLOSING (See page 25)

Day 26

I am the LORD your God;
sanctify yourselves therefore,
and be holy, for I am holy.
Leviticus 11:44

As he who called you is holy,
be holy yourselves in all your conduct.
1 Peter 1:15

Today we consider what it means to say that the church is holy.

There is much misunderstanding about the meaning of the term "holy." Too many seem to think it means entirely good, without flaw. That may serve us well when speaking of a holy God. But a perfect church? Hardly. At root, holiness instead has to do with being set apart, indeed with being different. In the commandments, when God called for one day a week to be holy, God meant that this day was to be set aside as different from the other six, distinctive in its practices. So also the Hebrew people were to exhibit holiness by refusing to bow down to the idols worshiped by all of the neighboring nations. Similarly, the church is called to live out in the world ways of being and doing that are alternatives to accustomed standards and customs.

This means that, far from being embarrassed when its ideals are at odds with accepted ways, the Christian community should revel in what it distinctively has to offer to the world. When the lives of people are being ruined by oppression and the church protests, we are exemplifying holiness. When greed goes unchecked, even applauded, and Christian people cry out "Enough!" we should rejoice that we are fulfilling our calling to be different for the sake of what is right. How willing are we to be considered out of step with society in order to be holy? Who wants to be labeled as "odd," after all? But we are called to be a holy church, not a club that panders to whatever is currently popular.

OPENING PRAYER
O God, our help and our hope:
Holy is your name,

84

unlike every other name we know.
Holy are your ways,
  beyond the reach of earthly imperfection.
Holy are your people,
  called by you to show the world
    a new way, a new hope.
Cause us to be what you call us to be;
through Jesus Christ,
  who died for being different. Amen.

CENTERING (See pages 19-21 for suggested ways of centering.)

PRAYER FOR ILLUMINATION
First, O Lord, the reading of the words.
Then the silence, seeking the Word beyond all words.
Finally, holy God, obedience to that Word. Amen.

PSALM 84:1-8 (Year One)
        84:8-12 (Year Two)

SCRIPTURE READINGS FOR THE DAY (See pages 179-215)

CONTEMPLATION (See page 23)

ACTS APPROPRIATE TO THE DAY OF THE WEEK (See pages 103-6)

ACTS APPROPRIATE TO THE TIME OF THE YEAR (See pages 107-34)

ACTS APPROPRIATE TO THE OCCASION (See pages 135-58)

THE PRAYER OF THE WHOLE CHURCH (See pages 156-57)

CLOSING (See page 25)

Day 27

People will come
from east and west, from north and south,
and will eat in the kingdom of God.
Luke 13:29

Make disciples of all nations,
baptizing them in the name
of the Father and of the Son and of the Holy Spirit,
and teaching them to obey everything that I have commanded you.
Matthew 28:19-20

Today we consider what it means to say that the church is catholic.

Few words have occasioned so much misunderstanding as this one. Some churches that use the Apostles' Creed or Nicene Creed refuse to follow the standard wording, and instead of saying "catholic" they say "Christian" or "universal." The second of the alternatives is the correct one. "Catholic," far from meaning one particular branch of the church, means the entire tree of the church, so to speak. (The Roman Catholic Church is that part of the universal church headquartered in Rome. But Protestant bodies could well argue that they are "Lutheran Catholics" or "Presbyterian Catholics," for example.)

To affirm the catholicity of the church is to remind ourselves that our sisters and brothers in the faith are scattered across the whole earth, using various languages, liturgies, and customs; but all give allegiance to Jesus Christ as God's messenger of grace and peace. Too often we focus so much attention on the work of our own congregation or denomination that we lose sight of the church catholic. To the extent that we do this, we diminish our appreciation for the diversity of the Christian family.

OPENING PRAYER
   Let all the peoples praise you, O God;
   let all the peoples praise you.
      For you have created all, and redeemed all.
      You have established a church,

calling it to be faithful in every time and place.
Draw together all who are one in Christ,
 that across the whole earth
  there may be witnesses to you,
to the glory of your Name,
 O God, One in diversity,
 O God, Three in unity. Amen.

CENTERING (See pages 19-21 for suggested ways of centering.)

PRAYER FOR ILLUMINATION
 In every time and place, O God,
 send forth your Spirit to instruct your people,
  that the Scriptures may come alive
   as they are read and contemplated
    in thoughtful adoration.
 Grant this in the name of Jesus. Amen.

PSALM 65:1-8 (Year One)
   67 (Year Two)

SCRIPTURE READINGS FOR THE DAY (See pages 179-215)

CONTEMPLATION (See page 23)

ACTS APPROPRIATE TO THE DAY OF THE WEEK (See pages 103-6)

ACTS APPROPRIATE TO THE TIME OF THE YEAR (See pages 107-34)

ACTS APPROPRIATE TO THE OCCASION (See pages 135-58)

THE PRAYER OF THE WHOLE CHURCH (See pages 156-57)

CLOSING (See page 25)

Day 28

As you have sent me into the world,
so I have sent them into the world.
John 17:18

You are citizens with the saints
and also members of the household of God,
built upon the foundation of the apostles and prophets,
with Christ Jesus himself as the cornerstone.
Ephesians 2:19-20

Today we consider what it means to say that the church is apostolic.

In its broadest sense, an apostle is a person who is sent on a mission. In this sense all Christians are apostles. Some churches refer to their missionary efforts as "the apostolate." But early in the life of the church certain persons became such noted and effective communicators of the gospel that they came to be called "*the* apostles," almost as if there were no others. Although often limited to the Twelve together with Paul, even in a narrow sense more should be included than that. It can well be argued, for example, that the first apostles were Mary Magdalene and "the other Mary," since they specifically were sent by the risen Lord to tell the others that he had triumphed over death. (See Matthew 28:7.)

The church is apostolic in both senses. All Christians are sent into the world to proclaim the good news. But always they are to measure their understanding against "the apostolic faith"—that which was set forth by those who were closest to Jesus. We who are sent in our own day are not free to invent a "new" gospel. Our task is to find new ways of proclamation, well suited to our time and place in history, so that our contemporaries can grasp the meaning in this age of what the hymn writer Katherine Hankey called "the old, old story of Jesus and his love."

This is why the content of the Bible is fixed. It records the earliest memories of Jesus. We are not free to add to Scripture our own experiences, as if they, too, were sacred history; but we are responsible for translating into understandable terms anything in the Scriptures that cannot be readily grasped by people in our day. And this translation will take into account our own experiences. This is what it means to say that the church is apostolic.

OPENING PRAYER
To you, O God, be all glory.
From you we have received grace upon grace.
To you we owe all allegiance and gratitude.
In the midst of the temptations, distractions,
    and glamour of the world,
fasten our attention on the faith
    we have received from others
    and are called to share with others.
Make us your true apostles,
through Christ, who summons and sends us. Amen.

CENTERING (See pages 19-21 for suggested ways of centering.)

PRAYER FOR ILLUMINATION
Holy God,
    because it is your desire to be proclaimed
        to all the world,
grant us clarity of understanding
    as we search the Scriptures;
and teach us how best
    we can communicate their message
        to those who know it not;
through Christ our risen Savior. Amen.

PSALM 96:1-9 (Year One)
        96:10-13 (Year Two)

SCRIPTURE READINGS FOR THE DAY (See pages 179-215)

CONTEMPLATION (See page 23)

ACTS APPROPRIATE TO THE DAY OF THE WEEK (See pages 103-6)

ACTS APPROPRIATE TO THE TIME OF THE YEAR (See pages 107-34)

ACTS APPROPRIATE TO THE OCCASION (See pages 135-58)

THE PRAYER OF THE WHOLE CHURCH (See pages 156-57)

CLOSING (See page 25)

Day 29

In hope we were saved.
Now hope that is seen is not hope.
For who hopes for what is seen?
But if we hope for what we do not see,
we wait for it with patience.
Romans 8:24-25

For through the Spirit,
by faith, we eagerly wait
for the hope of righteousness.
Galatians 5:5

Today we consider the hope eternal.

The church that carefully reads its New Testament always looks toward the future. Indeed we believe that what we hope for in the future should shape how we live in the present. Otherwise why do we say continually, and on the authority of Jesus: "Your will be done on earth as in heaven"?

Our hope for heaven is neither wishful thinking nor delusion. It is the firm conviction that in spite of all the evils that beset us, God is in charge, and in the end the triumph of God will be made clear and we will share in its glory. Meanwhile, the one holy catholic and apostolic church is to live out on earth the hope to which it clings. Thus, insofar as possible, the church is to love the world in the same way that "God so loved the world."

To do so is to avoid two dangerous extremes: dreading the future as a time of terror, on the one hand, and, on the other, yearning so much for a better future that the present seems oppressive. Our hope eternal is characterized neither by fear nor by escapism. It is founded on the rock of divine goodness and faithfulness that undergirds both the transient life of this world and unending life in the nearer presence of God hereafter.

OPENING PRAYER
Grant to me, gracious God,
and to all of my sisters and brothers in Christ,

so strong a sense of your steadfast love
that we may see in what you promise us
    both a firm hope for the future and
    a pattern of life we can follow in the present;
through Jesus Christ our Lord. Amen.

CENTERING (See pages 19-21 for suggested ways of centering.)

PRAYER FOR ILLUMINATION
    God, the help and confidence of all who seek you:
    without your aid I confront the Scriptures
        with eyes that do not see,
        with ears that do not hear,
        with a heart that will not learn or love.
    Open my eyes and ears and heart in these moments,
        and cause me to know inwardly
        what you present to me outwardly;
    through Jesus Christ, who opens and none can shut. Amen.

PSALM 42 (Year One)
        46 (Year Two)

SCRIPTURE READINGS FOR THE DAY (See pages 179-215)

CONTEMPLATION (See page 23)

ACTS APPROPRIATE TO THE DAY OF THE WEEK (See pages 103-6)

ACTS APPROPRIATE TO THE TIME OF THE YEAR (See pages 107-34)

ACTS APPROPRIATE TO THE OCCASION (See pages 135-58)

THE PRAYER OF THE WHOLE CHURCH (See pages 156-57)

CLOSING (See page 25)

Day 30*

Were not ten made clean?
But the other nine, where are they?
Was none of them found to return and give praise to God
except this foreigner?
Luke 17:17-18

O give thanks to the LORD, for he is good;
for his steadfast love endures forever.
Who can utter the mighty doings of the LORD,
or declare his praise?
Happy are those who observe justice,
who do righteousness at all times.
Psalm 106:1-3

Today we consider thanksgiving to God, both in word and deed.

Ingratitude is a grave offense against God, and the closer to God we think we are, the more we are inclined to take divine grace for granted. So Jesus suggests in Luke 17:11-19. For this reason, even the practice of daily devotions can be dangerous!

The psalmist, quoted above, points out another difficulty in giving thanks. We do not have sufficient words to praise God's goodness. Oral testimony is important, to be sure. But to it we are to add the observance of justice, the doing of righteousness at all times. Otherwise our voices sound like "a noisy gong or a clanging cymbal" (1 Corinthians 13:1).

As this month draws to its close, ask:

> For what experiences in the past month
>   do I particularly praise God?
> What opportunities for thanksgiving
>   have I overlooked during this month?
> Have I shown gratitude in words only,

---

*Note that in April, June, September, and November the materials for Day 30 are not used. Instead use the materials for "Final Day." (In February Days 29 and 30 are deleted in leap years, as are Days 28-30 in all other years.)

or also by my deeds—
by my demonstrated concern
for the weak, the lowly, the suffering?

OPENING PRAYER
Bless the Lord, O my soul.
All that is within me: Bless God's holy name.
For you, O God, have showered me
with blessings too numerous to count;
in return, too often I have overlooked,
or taken for granted your bounty.
Beyond all else that you have given,
grant me yet one thing more:
an unfailingly grateful heart. Amen.

CENTERING (See pages 19-21 for suggested ways of centering.)

PRAYER FOR ILLUMINATION
O God, there is nowhere that you are not.
You fill every crevice of the universe.
Therefore through the reading and study of your word,
infiltrate my whole being with your grace
until no part of me is exempt
from seeking and serving you;
through Christ, who is all in all. Amen.

PSALM 69:30-36 (Year One)
92:1-5 (Year Two)

SCRIPTURE READINGS FOR THE DAY (See pages 179-215)

CONTEMPLATION (See page 23)

ACTS APPROPRIATE TO THE DAY OF THE WEEK (See pages 103-6)

ACTS APPROPRIATE TO THE TIME OF THE YEAR (See pages 107-34)

ACTS APPROPRIATE TO THE OCCASION (See pages 135-58)

THE PRAYER OF THE WHOLE CHURCH (See pages 156-57)

CLOSING (See page 25)

Final Day

Examine yourselves,
and only then eat of the bread and drink of the cup.
For all who eat and drink without discerning the body,
eat and drink judgment against themselves.
1 Corinthians 11:28-29

Search me, O God, and know my heart;
test me and know my thoughts.
See if there is any wicked way in me,
and lead me in the way everlasting.
Psalm 139:23-24

Today we engage in end-of-the-month self-evaluation.

The passage from 1 Corinthians quoted above has often been misunderstood as a warning against receiving Holy Communion. Paul does make this statement after criticizing the Corinthians' practices at the common meal. But his concern is that their malpractice reflected a failure to understand what it is to be a community of faith in which each one cares for and about all of the others. Their selfishness while at table created a situation in which the poor (who arrived late after a hard day of work) found that all of the food at the evening meal had already been eaten by the affluent. Paul asserted that this betrayed the fact that the congregation at Corinth did not discern what it means to be "the body of Christ." Therefore, profound self-examination was in order.

Our communion practices are quite different, but the need for periodic self-evaluation is no less necessary in other areas of our lives. The final day of the month provides a convenient schedule for such examination, found in today's order below.

This day can be an occasion for fasting or abstinence for those who have no illnesses that forbid such practices. Fasting may mean forgoing food and drink (except for water and perhaps juices) for part of a day or an entire day. Abstinence may mean being a vegetarian for a day, if ordinarily you are not. Such practices are ways of indicating to God our seriousness about self-discipline.

In addition, fasting reveals how much time and attention we normally give to food; the time not used for these activities today can be devoted to prayer and to the kind of extended self-examination suggested below. Finally, fasting enables us to identify with those who are perpetually hungry; many Christians contribute to the poor the money saved when not eating.

Because Sunday perpetually commemorates the resurrection of the Lord, the church has taught that the Lord's Day can never be a fast day; when Sunday is the closing day of the month, Saturday or Monday may be used as a fast day instead. It has also been the custom to exclude fasting throughout the entire Great Fifty Days—from Easter Day through the Day of Pentecost.

Those who cannot or prefer not to fast may find other ways to make this a distinctive day at the close of every month, such as by giving up watching television for the day and reading the Bible or other edifying literature instead.

Because no form of self-examination can be devised that fits everyone, you will undoubtedly wish to evaluate yourself in areas not listed below. Therefore following this order, two pages are intentionally left blank. You are encouraged to write there those things concerning which you wish to evaluate yourself month after month, by way of setting goals for spiritual growth.

OPENING PRAYER
> Give me honesty and integrity, O Lord,
>> that I may carefully probe both my actions
>> and my motivations
> with a view to reforming those
>> that are in need of remedy.
> Help me to put aside self-deception and defensiveness,
>> and to acknowledge that I am indeed a sinner,
>> yet one who knows the power of grace
>> and covets the joy of transformation.
> Search me and know my heart,
>> and lead me in the way everlasting;
> through Christ, who died for our sins
>> and rose for our justification. Amen.

CENTERING (See pages 19-21 for suggested ways of centering.)

PRAYER FOR ILLUMINATION
Show me through the Scriptures, O God,
both your judgment and your grace,
that I may be
neither self-satisfied with my works
nor terrified by your wrath.
Enable me to accept Jesus
as both my example of all goodness
and the redeemer of all of my sin.
For in him and through him I pray. Amen.

PSALM 26 (Year One)
150 (Year Two)

SCRIPTURE READINGS FOR THE DAY (See pages 179-215)

CONTEMPLATION (See page 23)

SELF-EXAMINATION
In the month now ended:

To what extent have I identified God's work in my life:
in making me more compassionate toward
the needs of individuals?
in giving me resolve to do what I can
to remedy the deep ills of society,
particularly all forms of abuse and exploitation
that demean God's daughters and sons?
in giving me greater spiritual discernment
while at prayer,
particularly in the study of the Scriptures?

Have I prayed earnestly for peace, and given thanks
for all who seek to bring it about?
How have I worked toward it in my own community?
in my own family?

To what extent have I worked to preserve and protect
the physical world around me,
by conserving its resources

and refraining from those practices
    which upset its delicate balances of life?

To what extent have I during this past month
    participated in the ministries of the congregation
       to which I belong,
    or of other religious groups within my community?

How have I supported those in sorrow, pain, and confusion,
    and others who are distraught?
    Those who have suffered from natural disasters?

What support have I given
    to new members in the congregation,
    particularly to those who at their baptism I promised,
       together with the whole people of God in this place,
    to nurture and undergird with prayer?

Am I more aware now than before
    of the extent of the church across the whole earth
    and of the many problems faced by fellow Christians?

Have I been faithful in both
    the private and public worship of God?

In the longer range:

    Looking beyond the month just ended,
    what growth do I see in my walk with God across the years?
    What threats to committed discipleship have I overcome?
    What threats still challenge me?
    What growth in grace do I wish to achieve in the future?

    Have I remembered to give thanks to God
       for all progress I see
    and to seek earnestly from God
       the power to follow more fully?

PRAYER AT THE CLOSE OF SELF-EXAMINATION
O God, mercifully forgive
the wrong I have done
and the good I have neglected to do.
But let not your forgiveness be used by me
as an excuse to continue in my old ways.
Rather, let your kindness alter what I am and do.
Restore in me the image of yourself
with which you endowed me at creation.

Lord, have mercy upon me, a sinner.
Christ, have mercy upon me, a penitent.
Lord, have mercy upon me, and make me whole. Amen.

ACTS APPROPRIATE TO THE DAY OF THE WEEK (See pages 103-6)

ACTS APPROPRIATE TO THE TIME OF THE YEAR (See pages 107-34)

ACTS APPROPRIATE TO THE OCCASION (See pages 135-58)

THE PRAYER OF THE WHOLE CHURCH (See pages 156-57)

CLOSING (See page 25)

This page is blank so that you may record here your own needs for self-examination.

This page is blank so that you may record here your own needs for self-examination.

II. Acts Appropriate to the Day of the Week

The Lord's Day

God of great deeds:
On the first day of the week you wondrously
   called forth light out of darkness.
On the first day of the week you graciously
   raised Jesus from the dead.
On the first day of the week you powerfully
   formed the church through the gift
     of your Holy Spirit.
By this triple witness you testify to us
   concerning your covenant love.
Grant that all who worship you this day
   may do so in spirit and in truth
and present to you a living sacrifice
   of praise and thanksgiving;
through Christ our Savior. Amen.

Monday

Remember, O Lord, all for whom we prayed
   while gathered yesterday in public worship.
Teach us how best we may serve them
   with deeds of love and kindness.
Forgive us for any whom we neglected in prayer;
   help us to open our hearts to the needs of all.
Grant that what you taught us to do
   we may both ponder and perform.

[If the Lord's Supper was received, add this:]
We bless you for the signs of your love
    revealed in bread and cup.
By these gifts grant us not only hope
    until we gather at the heavenly banquet,
but also graciousness that we may share with others
    among us the fruits of this earth.

*[If persons yesterday made profession of faith through
baptism, confirmation, or reaffirmation, add this:]*
Make firm and steadfast the faith of those
    who yesterday made covenant promises
        in the midst of the congregation,
            that they may be worthy disciples.
Remind us continually to keep the promises
    we have made to them
        as sisters and brothers in Christ Jesus.

[In all cases conclude the prayer as follows:]
Bind into one company of hope
    and one community of service
all that you have made and redeemed
by the sacrificial life and death of Jesus,
    our risen Lord. Amen.

Tuesday

God, our rock and our salvation:
    undergird us with your strength,
lest we fail because we rely
    upon ourselves alone.
Assist us with your Holy Spirit
    that we may abide in your love
    and trust in your grace.
Spread upon us your transforming power;
overpower us with your good will
    and forgiveness
offered to us and to all
    through Christ our savior. Amen.

Wednesday

In the middle of this week, good Lord,
    assure me again of your presence
    in the midst of life.
Renew my strength and determination
    to do your will on earth,
        even as it is done in heaven.
Save me from self-contentment,
    from a vision that is too narrow.
Enable me to reach
    beyond my parish, into my community;
    beyond my community, into every corner
        of your anguished world.
Help me to see even beyond this world
        into the vast expanses of your universe,
    created as a sign of your extraordinary love
        and of your enduring power.
This I ask through Christ,
    through whom all things were made,
    in whom all things hold together. Amen.

Thursday

God, your glory calls your people
        to adoration daily.
Guide and inspire all who plan
and who will take leadership
    in the worship of our congregation
when again we gather in prayer
        on the Lord's Day.
To musicians, lectors, preachers, and all others,
    give a full measure of your Holy Spirit,
    that they may glorify not themselves but you.
Prepare my heart
and the hearts of all of your people
    to receive their ministries
with joy and gratitude to you,
    and extravagant generosity toward others.
This we pray through Christ, the Risen One. Amen.

Friday

On this day, Lord Jesus,
the flesh which you took upon yourself
for us and for our salvation
was hanged by us upon the cross.
There you suffered all things
and died that we might have life
and have it in the abundance
of your astounding grace.
Blessed are you, Lord Jesus,
with the Father and the Holy Spirit,
one God, throughout time and all eternity. Amen.

Saturday

Prepare our hearts, O Lord,
to join together with your whole congregation
to praise and serve you.
Reveal your presence to all who will gather
in adoration and self-offering.
To those who cannot for good reason
go gladly into your house,
give your strength and consolation,
that they may know of the concern
of their communities of faith.
Make us receptive to your word for us,
and enable us to know and do your will.
Bind your people together in
a shared faith, a common witness,
and compassionate service to the world;
through Jesus our Savior. Amen.

III. Acts Appropriate to the Time of the Year

Advent

Introduction

Because the season of Advent begins on the fourth Sunday prior to December 25, it is often mistakenly thought of primarily as a time to ready ourselves for the observance of Christmas. In fact, Advent is first of all about the future, about the Christian hope for a new heaven and a new earth as a gift from God. It is tied to Christmas because it is in the person and work of Jesus that we glimpse (as fully as humans are able) what God has in mind for the future. Jesus is in a true sense a picture of the future.

For that future we are to wait in hope. We are to pray for its coming, as The Lord's Prayer teaches us to do. (The word "advent" means "coming.") Above all we are to wrestle with this truth: Although we have in our minds ideas about what God's final reign will be like, these may be as imperfect as the ancient hope that Messiah would come as a military leader to overthrow Rome. When Messiah came, his birth and life were so unlike what was expected that even many devout persons missed the point. So we also are in danger of doing the same if our understanding of God's final reign of righteousness is so tightly closed that we give God no freedom to work in divinely appointed ways that may mystify us and that certainly will surprise us with their newness.

Prayers for Advent

> Stir up our hearts, O God,
> to prepare ourselves to receive your Son.

Grant that when he comes and knocks
   he will not find us sleeping in sin,
but awake to righteousness,
endlessly rejoicing in his love.
So purify our hearts and minds
   that we may be ready to receive
   his promise of life eternal. Amen.

Galesian Sacramentary, ca. 500

O come, thou radiant Morning Star,
   again in human darkness shine!
Arise resplendent from afar!
   assert thy royalty divine:
thy sway o'er all the earth maintain,
and now begin thy glorious reign. Amen.

Charles Wesley (1707–1788)
English clergyman and poet

God, our help through all that has been,
   our hope through all that will be:
In every season of our lives you come to us,
   offering us the fullness of your life.
You call us to await the day
   when all things shall be fulfilled
     in the joy of your eternal reign.
Grant therefore to me, and to all of your people, patience—
now, as we approach Christmas Day,
   and always, as we approach the day
     on which you shall destroy unrighteousness
     and cause justice to reign over us all.
Your kingdom come, your will be done on earth as in heaven.
Amen.

Advent and Christian Hope

"Hope that is seen is not hope" (Romans 8:24). We do not know what the future holds. We do not know if God's reign will commence in one week or in one billion years. We do not know how earthly history fits in the monumental scheme of cosmic history. We do not even know the hour of our own death, much less the day of our resurrection. But we live in hope. Hope, because we believe that the God who has acted in the past, pre-eminently in Jesus, will act again. God is not done with creation, with Israel, with the church, or with us.... The Bible provides us with numerous models of hopeful expectation. The dreams, visions, and predictions it records are consistent on some levels and inconsistent on others. The latter fact cautions us against holding too-certain ideas about what lies ahead. We should remember that certainty about God's plan rendered some—including for a time the disciples themselves—incapable of recognizing Jesus. Faithfulness does not require such certainty, and easy certainty is a poor substitute for true faith. At its core [hope for the future] is about the character of God. If God can be trusted, then the future can be trusted with God.

That does not mean that [a hopeful] faith excuses passivity. To the contrary, the believer's vocation, insofar as possible, is to bring [hope for] the future into the present. If we anticipate justice, then let us live justly. If we anticipate the end of creation's groaning, then let us live today as healers of creation.... We are called to newness of life *now*. The values and priorities of God's dominion are believed only so far as they are enacted.

Craig C. Hill (1957–)
American New Testament scholar

The Hectic Pace of Advent as a Call to Confession

The pressures of scheduling that many people feel during Advent cause us to recall the opening words of a poem by William Wordsworth:

> The world is too much with us; late and soon,
> getting and spending, we lay waste our powers:
> Little we see in Nature that is ours.

As we rush from one social engagement to another, as we shop, and travel, and bake, and cook, and decorate, and send cards, and wrap gifts the world seems far too much with us. And yet, that world is the very world God loved so much as to send Jesus into it! So in some sense the world is not with us enough, if our getting and spending distract us from it.

Ironically, even the Advent tasks of the church can distract us:
the many services and the necessary preparation for them, the
added social gatherings within the congregation—even these can
put us further out of contact with the world God so loves. Thus
Advent may compel us to confess:

O Lord, in preparing to see you more fully
   we have allowed ourselves to be blinded
   to the presence we are already capable of recognizing.
Forgive us for putting second matters first,
   for being distracted rather than edified.
Remove from us all that competes with your way for us.
Quiet us down,
   that we may be still and know that you are God,
   that in silence we may hear your Word
      with new clarity
   and keep it
      with new intensity.
Grant this for the sake of Jesus,
   whom we would worship in spirit and in truth. Amen.

Christmas

Introduction

*Christmas is far more than one day on which to think about the birth
of a baby. It is a season that begins at sunset on December 24 and
extends forward to the time we call the Epiphany. Throughout this season we are to meditate on what it means to say that God came among us
in human form, to live and die as one of us. How can that be? How could
the Immortal become mortal? How could the Unseen become visible?
How could pure Spirit be revealed in physical flesh and blood? And why
would God want to do such a thing?*

*Until we have pondered these mysteries and allowed ourselves to be
awe-struck by their power, we will be prisoners to the custom of giving
gifts to relatives and friends without experiencing the One who is God's
Greatest Gift, given for the sake of all people of every time and place; we
will be gluttons who eat too much at Christmas festivities without par-*

taking in the exuberant joy of the Bread of Life first made known in Bethlehem (which means, "the place of bread").

Christmas is above all a season in which to say with the shepherds: "Let us go now to Bethlehem and see this thing that has taken place, which the Lord has made known to us" (Luke 2:15). It is a time also to return home, doing as the shepherds did: glorifying and praising God for all we have heard and seen.

Meditations for Christmas

How proper it is that Christmas should follow Advent—for [anyone] who looks toward the future, the Manger is situated on Golgotha, and the Cross has already been raised in Bethlehem.

Dag Hammarskjold (1905–1961)
Diplomat

In our own day a leading New Testament scholar, Father Raymond Brown, has warned us not to ruin Christmas with over-sentimentality. For, he insisted, in the nativity accounts themselves both Matthew and Luke present us with the fullness of the ministry of Jesus: He who is born for us must die at our hands. Even in the accounts of his birth, the passion story lies embedded.

This truth was articulated by the English poet and preacher John Donne. On Christmas Day, 1626, worshipers at St. Paul's Cathedral in London must have been startled when the dean of the cathedral began his sermon in this way:

"The whole life of Christ was a continual passion. Others die martyrs; but Christ was born a martyr. He found a Golgotha [where he was crucified] even in Bethlehem, where he was born. For, to his tenderness then, the straws were almost as sharp as the thorns after, and the manger as uneasy at first as his cross at last. His birth and his death were but one continual act; and his Christmas Day and his Good Friday are but the evening and morning of one and the same day. And even as his birth is his death, so every action and passage that manifests Christ to us is his birth."

Prayer for the Season of Christmas

What is this jewel that is so precious?
I can see that it has been quarried,

not by mortals,
    but by God.
It is you, dear Jesus.
You have been dug from the rocks of heaven itself
    to be offered to me as a gift beyond price.
You shine in the darkness.
Every color of the rainbow can be seen within you.
The whole earth is bathed in your light.
Infant Jesus, by being born as one of us
    you have taken upon yourself the pain of death.
But such a jewel can never be destroyed.
You are immortal.
And by defying your own death,
    you shall deliver me from death.

Adam of St. Victor, died 1177
Monk of the Abbey of St. Victor in Paris

For Meditation and Confession at Christmas

Yet if his Majesty, our sovereign lord,
should of his own accord
friendly himself invite,
and say, "I'll be your guest tomorrow night,"
how we should stir ourselves, call and command
all hands to work: "Let no man idle stand!

"Set me fine Spanish tables in the hall;
see they be fitted all;
Let there be room to eat
and order taken that there want no meat.
See every sconce and candlestick made bright,
that without tapers they may give a light.

"Look to the presence: Are the carpets spread,
the dazie o'er the head,
the cushions in the chairs,
and all the candles lighted on the stairs?
Perfume the chambers, and in any case
let each man give attendance in his place!"

Thus, if a king were coming, would we do;
and 'twere good reason too;
for 'tis a duteous thing
to show all honor to an earthly king,
and after all our travail and our cost,
so he be pleased, to think no labor lost.

But at the coming of the King of Heaven
all's set at six and seven;
we wallow in our sin,
Christ cannot find a chamber in the inn.
We entertain him always like a stranger,
and, as at first, still lodge him in the manger.

Manuscript found at Christ Church, England

Christmas Poem: "A Child My Choice"

Let folly praise that fancy loves,
I praise and love that Child,
whose heart no thought, whose tongue no word,
whose hand no deed defiled.
I praise him most, I love him best,
all praise and love is his:
While I him love, I in him live,
and cannot live amiss.

Love's sweetest mark, laud's highest theme,
man's most desired light,
to love him life, to leave him death,
to live in him delight.
He mine by gift, I his by debt,
this each to other due;
first friend he was, best friend he is,
all times will try him true.

Though young, yet wise; though small, yet strong;
though man, yet God he is;
as wise he knows, as strong he can,
as God he loves to bliss.
His knowledge rules, his strength defends,

his love doth cherish all;
his birth our joy, his life our light,
his death our end of thrall.

Alas! he weeps, he sighs, he pants,
yet do his angels sing;
out of his tears, his sighs, his throbs
doth bud a joyful spring.
Almighty Babe, whose tender arms
can force all foes to fly:
Correct my faults, protect my life,
direct me when I die.

Robert Southwell (1561?–1595)
Hanged, drawn, and quartered
for serving as a Jesuit priest
in Protestant England

Christmas Poem: "Thou Didst Leave Thy Throne"

Thou didst leave thy throne and thy kingly crown,
  when thou camest to earth for me;
but in Bethlehem's home there was found no room
  for thy holy nativity.
    O come to my heart, Lord Jesus;
    there is room in my heart for thee.

Heaven's arches rang when the angels sang,
  proclaiming thy royal decree;
but in lowly birth didst thou come to earth,
  and in great humility.
    O come to my heart, Lord Jesus.
    There is room in my heart for thee.

The foxes found rest and the birds their nest
  in the shade of the forest tree;
but thy couch was the sod, O thou Son of God,
  in the deserts of Galilee.
    O come to my heart, Lord Jesus.
    There is room in my heart for thee.
Thou cam'st, O Lord, with the living word

that should set thy people free;
but with mocking scorn and with crown of thorn
   they bore thee to Calvary.
     O come to my heart, Lord Jesus.
     There is room in my heart for thee.

When heaven's arches shall ring and her choir shall sing
   at thy coming to victory,
let thy voice call me home, saying:
     "Yet there is room. There is room at my side for thee!"
     And my heart shall rejoice, Lord Jesus,
       when thou comest and callest me.

Emily E. S. Elliott, 1836–1897

Silence in Heaven: An Imaginative Account

Revelation 8:1 reports that when the Lamb of God opened the seventh seal of the sacred book, "there was silence in heaven for about half an hour."

But imagine events in heaven long before this, before the birth of Jesus. An edict had gone throughout the courts of God announcing that a full assembly of the hosts of the Lord was to be convened. All were to attend: the angels and the archangels, the seraphim and the cherubim, the entire company of heaven. The summons aroused great curiosity, for this was not a normal event in the celestial schedule. What could God want? Certainly neither the advice nor the consent of the hosts of heaven. God, being all-wise, has no need of counselors. God, being all-good and all-powerful, does not require anyone to ratify divine decisions. So why this convocation? What business was to be transacted?

When the appointed day arrived, all assembled precisely on time around the throne. With respect equal to their curiosity, they anxiously awaited the proceedings. A hush fell over the eager crowd as a voice came from the throne:

"You know the events that have taken place of late on the planet Earth," said God. Yes, they knew all too well. The earthlings had been notorious for their willful disobedience against their Creator. Adam and Eve paid no heed to the clear command of God. Their son Cain rose up and brutally slew his own brother

Abel, and things went downhill from there. Yes, they all knew the sorry history of life on earth.

God continued: "I have sent judges and monarchs and prophets to the people whom I love. Those whom I have appointed have corrected and admonished and warned their fellow human beings, but to no avail. The children of earth simply will not listen to their own kind. Therefore a new strategy must be devised. Someone from here must go down to them, someone who carries divine authority, so that finally they will listen and obey, so that finally they will grasp the depth of my loving concern for them."

At this word the heavenly assembly began to be agitated. They surmised that God was about to ask for volunteers, or even to conscript one or more of them for this odious task. They knew all too well the mess on earth, and the stubborness that characterized the human race.

Then the voice came from the throne again: "Whom shall we send? Who will go for us?" No angelic being dared look at any other, let alone look toward the throne. With unease and embarrassment each one stared at the ground or looked vacantly into space, standing on one foot and then the other in their dismay. Minutes passed. No word was said. Once again the voice of God was heard: "Whom shall we send? Who will go for us?" Once again there was no response. Not one volunteer was to be found.

One more time God spoke: "Then I shall myself go and dwell among them, as one of them, born into their midst." A great gasp filled the air, until the very pillars of heaven seemed to quake. Had they heard correctly? Surely not! God would go? God would not only visit that miserable place but would actually take on human flesh and blood and live among such scoundrels? No way! Could the Almighty Creator stoop to become a humble creature, the righteous Judge a friend of sinners? Why who knows what those humans would do? What if they did not recognize their celestial visitor as the Eternal One? Would they go so far even as to try to slay God-made-flesh? The thought was too horrible to contemplate.

Still, God would not lie or jest about matters so serious. They must have heard correctly: "I shall myself go and dwell among them, as one of them, born into their midst." It was too much to take in, even for angels. And so there was a stunned silence in heaven for about half an hour.

The Epiphany and Baptism of the Lord

Introduction

"Epiphany" is a Greek term that means "manifestation" or "revelation." It refers particularly to the way Jesus was made known to all, especially to the Gentiles. Traditionally observed on January 6, it is now usually celebrated on the Sunday prior, unless January 6 is itself a Sunday.

The Epiphany reveals the identity of Jesus by exploring the question: "Who is this who has been born in a stable and is on his way to the cross?" In part the answer lies hidden in the gifts the magi presented: This is the King of kings. (Monarchs owned most of the gold in the ancient world.) This is God with us. (Incense was burned in many religions to signify the presence of the deity.) This is the one who suffers and dies. (Myrrh was both administered as a pain killer and used in embalming.) But the place of origin of the magi was also crucial to the identity of Jesus. Luke's story of the nativity establishes that Jesus is made known to the Jews (in the persons of the shepherds and of Simeon and Anna in Luke 2). Matthew extends the manifestation to Gentiles from the East. Therefore Christ is the One who has come for the salvation of all peoples.

A Prayer for the Epiphany

O God,
 you made of one blood all nations,
  and, by a star in the East,
   revealed to all peoples him whose name is Emmanuel.
Enable us who know your presence with us
  so to proclaim his unsearchable riches
   that all may come to his light
    and bow before the brightness of his rising,
who lives and reigns with you and the Holy Spirit,
  now and forever. Amen.

117

Prayer for the Sunday of the Lord's Baptism

By word and sign, O God,
    you identified Jesus at his baptism
that we might know him to be
    your Beloved One,
    the vessel of your goodness.
By that same grace
    you have united us in Christ
    and called us your people.
How dimly we understand such love!
Deepen our faith.
Intensify our zeal.
Unite the separated branches of your church
    that we may bear an undivided witness
    before the world.
Through Jesus Christ,
    in whom you are pleased to dwell. Amen.

Lent

Introduction

Lent began as a time of final intense preparation for those adults who were to be baptized at Easter and as a time of renewed spiritual intensity among all who had previously been baptized. In imitation of Jesus' sojourn of forty days and nights in the desert, it came to be a season of forty fast days. Sundays were excluded since the Lord's Day, being a perpetual commemoration of the joy of his victory over death, can never be a fast day. Therefore Lent begins on a Wednesday, named for the ashes placed on the foreheads of the faithful both as a sign of repentance and as a reminder that we have come from dust and will return to dust.

Therefore Lent is a journey from death to resurrection: from the natural death we have earned through our sins to the gift of life we can never merit but which God nevertheless offers us in Christ who dies for us and with us, who joins us to himself in his victory over death.

A Prayer for Use Throughout Lent

God of all good life,
    on our journey toward Easter,

cleanse our hearts of every desire to mimic
   the violence of wrongs that befall us.
Save us from becoming the evil we hate.
Save us from denial of abuses which daily crucify Christ afresh.
Drive away
   the chilling cold, the wintry frost of numbing detachment
     from others' pain,
   and our own hurts, also.
Breathe, O breathe your empowering Spirit
   into the troubled hearts of your children
     who wish they could wish to love but cannot.

Creator of our bodies, Father and Mother of our spirits,
   how we yearn to see you and our friend Jesus face to face.
Precious to us are the Christ-like influences,
     and the whispered encouragement to keep on keeping on,
   of souls whom we have loved long since and lost awhile.
What a morning it will be when
     we mingle our voices with theirs,
   and with all the souls invisible,
     and adoring angels in a mighty chorus of unending wonder.
My Lord, what a morning when you shall crown us
   with the crowns you are holding now above our heads.
Chastise, charm and enchant us
   until we have grown tall enough to wear them.
Hear our prayer in the name of Jesus,
   the Shining Way, the Truth, and the Life. Amen.

Obie Wright, Jr. (1944–)
Elder in the Baltimore-Washington Conference of
The United Methodist Church

Prayer for Ash Wednesday

Creator of all things:
You have made us from the dust of the earth.
You breathed into us your own vitality.
Yet each of us must one day render back to you
   the life we have on loan from you.
It shall be required of us that we lay down
   all of our pomp and pride

and return to dust.
So teach us to consider the brevity of our days
    that we may live them out with wisdom,
    as a people redeemed and made new
    by the power of the cross of Jesus. Amen.

An Ash Wednesday Meditation

In 1624 as communicable diseases ravaged London, John Donne, the poet and preacher, lay seriously ill in a home provided for him next to St. Paul's Cathedral of which he was then Dean. It was the custom of the day to toll the bell of the church whenever a member of that parish lay dying. The tolling bell called others to pray for the dying and their families. But first in each household or neighborhood, someone had to be sent to the church to ask for whom the bell was tolling. Thus Donne wrote his famous meditations on death.

Now, this bell tolling softly for another says to me: "Thou must die." Perchance he for whom the bell tolls may be so ill, as that he knows not it tolls for him. And perchance I may think myself so much better than I am, as that those who are about me and see my state may have caused it to toll for me, and I know not that.

The church is catholic, universal, and so are all of her actions. All that she does belongs to all. When she baptizes a child, that action concerns me; for the child is thereby connected to that body which is my head too and ingrafted into that body whereof I am a member. And when she buries a man, that action concerns me: all mankind is of one author and in one volume. When one man dies one chapter is not torn out of the book, but translated into a better language; and every chapter must be so translated.

God employs several translators. Some pieces are translated by age, some by sickness, some by war, some by justice; but God's hand is in every translation, and his hand shall bind up all our scattered leaves again for that library where every book shall lie open to one another.

As therefore the bell that rings to a sermon calls not upon the preacher only, but upon the congregation to come, so this bell calls us all; but how much more me, who am brought so near the door by this sickness....

No man is an island, entire of itself; every man is a piece of the continent, a part of the main. If a clod be washed away by the sea, Europe is the less, as well as if a promontory were, as well as if a manor of thy friend's or of thine own were. Any man's death diminishes me, because I am involved in mankind; and therefore never send to know for whom the bell tolls. It tolls for thee.

A Poem for Holy Week: "My Song Is Love Unknown"

My song is love unknown,
 my savior's love to me,
love to the loveless shown
 that they might lovely be.
  O who am I
   that for for my sake
   my Lord should take
  frail flesh and die?

He came from his blest throne
 salvation to bestow;
but men made strange, and none
 the longed for Christ would know.
  O my friend,
   my friend indeed,
   who at my need
  his life did spend.

Sometimes they strew his way,
 and his strong praises sing,
resounding all the day
 hosannas to their king;
  Then "Crucify!"
   is all their breath,
   and for his death
  they thirst and cry.

Why, what hath my Lord done?
 What makes this rage and spite?
He made the lame to run;
 he gave the blind their sight.

Sweet injuries!
  Yet they at these
    themselves displease,
  and 'gainst him rise.

They rise, and needs must have
  my dear Lord made away;
a murderer they save,
  the Prince of Life they slay.
    yet steadfast he
      to suffering goes,
      that he his foes
    from thence might free.

In life no house, no home
  my Lord on earth might have;
in death no friendly tomb
  but what a stranger gave.
    What may I say?
      Heaven was his home;
      but mine the tomb
    wherein he lay.

Here might I stay and sing,
  no story so divine.
Never was love, dear King,
  never was grief like thine.
    This is my friend,
      in whose sweet praise
      I all my days
    could gladly spend.

Samuel Crossman (1624–1683)
British poet

A Prayer for Palm-Passion Sunday

Jesus, on this day they hailed you with tree branches
  as you rode through Jerusalem;
  but shortly they would cry out against you
  and compel you to carry your own cross

through the same streets.
We confess that their fickleness is ours also,
    that infidelity to you lurks in our hearts
        as surely as it did in theirs.
By your graciousness grant that our songs of "Hosanna!"
    may not turn into shouts of "Crucify!"
By your cross and passion, save us, merciful Lord. Amen.

A Prayer for Holy Thursday

O God,
    your love was embodied in Jesus Christ,
        who washed his disciples' feet on the night of his betrayal.
Wash us from the stain of sin,
    so that, in the hours of danger,
we may not fail,
    but follow your Son through every trial,
        and praise him always as Lord and Christ,
        to whom be glory now and forever. Amen.

Presbyterian Church (U.S.A.) and
Cumberland Presbyterian Church

A Prayer for Good Friday

Savior of the world,
    what have you done to deserve this?
    And what have we done to deserve you?
Strung up between criminals,
cursed and spat upon,
    you wait for death,
    and look for us,
        for us whose sin has crucified you.

To the mystery of undeserved suffering,
    you bring the deeper mystery of unmerited love.
Forgive us for not knowing what we have done;
open our eyes to see what you are doing now,
    as, through wood and nails,
        you disempower our depravity
        and transform us by your grace. Amen.

Church of Scotland

A Prayer for the Eve of Easter

You have led us, O Lord,
   during the long weeks of Lent,
   on a journey through the wilderness.
Now we stand on tiptoe
   at the edge of glory and joy.
We do not ask that we should understand
   this great mystery of the Lord's resurrection
but only that we should enjoy it
   in ways that lead to greater faithfulness
      and more obedient witness to your gospel.
Enthrall your entire church with
   the wonders of your love
as we gather in worship to proclaim that
   Christ has died;
   Christ is risen;
   Christ will come again. Amen.

Easter: The Great Fifty Days

Introduction

What Easter celebrates is far too expansive to be confined to one day. So its message of joy is extended across fifty days, embracing eight Sundays; the first we call Easter Day and the final we know as the Day of Pentecost. In the ancient church both fasting and kneeling were forbidden as they were considered inappropriate to this season, and alleluias (banished from the liturgy throughout Lent) abounded, as they still do in our Easter hymns. (The six stanzas of Charles Wesley's beloved "Christ the Lord Is Risen Today" contain two dozen alleluias.)

The Gospels make clear that the resurrection of Jesus is no mere resuscitation (such as he had given to Lazarus, the daughter of Jairus, and the son of the widow of Nain, all of whom had to die again); nor is it a ghostly manifestation. Furthermore, it is not some psychological trick of wish fulfillment, as our current culture may be inclined to believe. The Resurrection is the manifestation of a new kind and quality of life, which we have no words to describe. If we think that we can understand it, we do not understand it at all. For resurrection is the sublime, mysterious gift of God, which we are to experience as both astounding and transforming.

The risen Christ is freed from the limitations of time and space, taken on at Bethlehem. That is the meaning of Ascension Day, the fortieth day of this season. The power of this Resurrection, mediated by the Holy Spirit, is what establishes and motivates the mission of the church. That is the meaning of the Pentecost, the fiftieth and final day.

An Address to Death

> Death: Be not proud, though some have called thee
> mighty and dreadful; for thou are not so.
> For those whom thou thinkest thou dost overthrow
> die not, poor Death; nor yet canst thou kill me.
> From rest and sleep (which but thy pictures be)
> much pleasure—then from thee much more must flow;
> and soonest our best men with thee do go:
> rest of their bones, and souls' delivery.
> Thou art slave to fate, chance, kings, and desperate men,
> and dost with poison, war, and sickness dwell;
> and poppy or charms can make us sleep as well—
> and better—than thy stroke. Why swell'st thou then?
> One short sleep past, we wake eternally,
> and death shall be no more. Death: Thou shalt die!

> *John Donne (1572–1631)*
> *English poet and clergyman*

A Meditation on the New Life in Christ

The resurrection of our Lord Jesus Christ points to a new life for those who believe in Jesus, and that is the mystery of his suffering and his resurrection—a fact that should loom larger and larger both in your awareness and in your conduct as Christ's people....

You want to be happy. I know that.... You seek after money because you think money will insure your well-being. But money does not make you happy.... You seek things in order to be happy, but no earthly thing can bring you happiness.

Had Jesus found happiness here on earth, you would find it also. Then what did he find when he came to you from another realm? He ate with you that which is abundant in the poor storehouse of earth; he drank vinegar and gall. But you Christ has invited to his sumptuous feast, the feast of heaven, the feast of angels, where he is himself the bread. Having come down from heaven and found here only the poor provisions of your earthly storehouse, he did not spurn your unworthy table, but invited you to his own. He who bore your misery, will he not also bestow blessings upon you?...

Therefore as long as we live in this decaying flesh, let us die with Christ by changing our conduct, so that we may live with Christ in love and uprightness. Until we come to him who came to us, until we begin to live with him who died for us, we shall not possess the blessed life.

Augustine of Hippo (354–430)
North African bishop
From a sermon to the newly baptized
during the week following Easter Day

A Prayer During the Great Fifty Days

Remembering thy resurrection, Lord Jesus, I worship thee,
    who art holy, who alone art without sin.
I fall down before thee, who wast crucified;
I praise and glorify thee, who art risen from the dead.
For thou alone art my God,
    and besides thee I know no other;
and of thy name alone will I make mention.
        Thou art risen indeed. Hallelujah!
Through thy glorious resurrection, O Lord Jesus,
    great joy has come to all thy people.
Wherefore I bless thee, O Lord;
    I celebrate thy blessed resurrection.
For thou hast abolished death,
    and brought life and immortality to light.
        Thou art risen indeed. Hallelujah!

Although thou wast laid in the grave, O thou Eternal,
    yet didst thou spoil the power of hell.
Thou didst rise victorious, O Christ my God,
    bringing resurrection
        to all that, living, believe in thee, and

to all that, dying, sleep in thee.
Thou art risen indeed. Hallelujah!

Henry Harbaugh (1817–1876), alt.
German-American Reformed pastor
and liturgical theologian

A Prayer for Ascension Day

Everliving God,
your eternal Christ once dwelt on earth,
    confined by time and space.
Give us faith to discern in every time and place
    the presence among us
    of him who is head over all things and fills all,
even Jesus Christ our ascended Lord. Amen.

A Prayer for the Day of Pentecost

We ask you, O Lord,
    by the fire of your Holy Spirit,
to set our hearts aflame with love, faith, and hope;
and blow through us with your holy wind,
    that we may proclaim your Gospel to others
    in ways which they can understand;
through Jesus Christ our Lord. Amen.

Based on the Gelasian Sacramentary,
an official prayer book of the church around A.D. 500.

A Meditation on the Varying Ministries of the Holy Spirit

There are some effects of the living power of the Holy Spirit which are invariable. When he dwells with a Christian soul, he invariably speaks in the voice of conscience; he speaks in the voice of prayer. He produces with the ease of a natural process, without effort, without the taint of self-consciousness, "love, joy, peace, long-suffering, gentleness, goodness, faith, meekness, temperance." Some of these graces must be found where he makes his home. There is no mistaking the atmosphere of his presence; in its main features it is the same now as in the days of the apostles. Just as in natural morality the main elements of "goodness" do not change, so in religious life....

127

But in the life of the individual Christian, or in that of the Church, there is legitimate room for irregular and exceptional forms of activity or excellence. Natural society is not strengthened by a stern repression of all that is peculiar in individual thought or practice; and this is not less true of spiritual or religious society. From the first, high forms of Christian excellence have often been associated with unconscious eccentricity. The eccentricity must be unconscious, because consciousness of eccentricity at once reduces it to a form of vanity which is entirely inconsistent with Christian excellence.

How many excellent Christians have been eccentric, deviating more or less from the conventional type of goodness which has been recognized by contemporary religious opinion. They pass away, and when they are gone we do justice to their characters; but while they are still with us, how hard do many of us find it to remember that there may be a higher reason for their peculiarities than we think. We know not the full purpose of each saintly life in the design of Providence; we know not much of the depths and heights whence it draws its inspiration; we can not tell when it cometh or whither it goeth. Only we know that he whose workmanship it is bloweth where he listeth.

Henry Parry Liddon (1829–1890)
Canon of St. Paul's Cathedral, London

Other Occasions of the Church's Year

A Prayer for Trinity Sunday (Sunday after the Day of Pentecost)

Holy God, merciful and mighty,
you dwell in a reality too deep for minds to fathom,
    in heights no human can attain.
You are Father, Son, and Breath Divine;
    and yet you are One God,
    undivided throughout eternity.
You are known, yet past all knowing,
    both Judge and Savior,
beyond the farthest edge of the universe,
    yet closer than hands and feet or breathing.
Blessed are you.
By the greatness that is yours alone,
    save your people. Amen.

A Prayer for All Saints' Day (First Sunday in November)

God of our ancestors,
God of generations yet unborn:
It is your will
so to fill us with your own Being,
so to forgive us even when we fail you,
that we may be called your holy people.
For the multitude of the faithful
whom we cannot remember
for the vastness of their number
and the distance of their days,
we bless your holy name.
For the multitude of the faithful
whom we do remember
because they have touched our lives
and given us instruction and inspiration,
we bless your holy name.

[Here you may pause to remember by name
the departed who have increased your faith.]

Receive them all into your arms of mercy.
Let light perpetual shine upon them,
and cause us to be numbered with them
in your everlasting glory,
through Jesus Christ our Lord. Amen.

A Prayer for the Sunday of Christ's Reign (Fifth Sunday prior to
December 25)

God, the ruler of all creation:
You sent Jesus to reign over us
from a cross, not a throne,
with a crown of thorns, not one of gold.
By this you teach us that your reign
is unlike any we might invent or envision.
At times we wonder whether
your reign is even a remote possibility,
for our world is filled with terrors;

so often you seem distant, even absent,
  powerless against the forces that intimidate us.
Yet, as Christ burst forth from a sepulcher,
  so also in your own good time
his astounding rule will have its way
  over every evil force and impulse.
This we believe, but help our unbelief.
Accept our feeble trust in your faithful triumph.
Support us with your strength
  until hope becomes sight
  and your future is fulfilled in all things. Amen.

THE CIVIL YEAR

At the Opening of a New Calendar Year

Almighty Father:
we pray thee graciously to lead us through
  the uncertainties of this new year
  of our earthly pilgrimage.
Protect us from the dangers of the way;
prepare us for the duties, the trials, the joys,
  and sorrows that await us;
and grant that each change the year brings with it
  may bring us nearer to thyself
  and to the eternal joy and rest that await the faithful
  in thy blessed and glorious presence;
through Jesus Christ our Lord. Amen.

Church of Scotland, 1952

For Martin Luther King, Jr., Day

O God of love, power, and justice,
  who wills the freedom and fulfillment of all your children:
We thank you for the constancy of your loving kindness
  and tender mercies toward us.
Especially on this day, as we celebrate the birthday and life
  of your servant and prophet, Dr. Martin Luther King, Jr.,
  we are reminded that in every age you raise up
  seers and sayers and doers of justice....

Because our needs are so great today and your care so constant,
  we know that you are rebuilding the network of compassion
    around new visionaries
    whom you have assembled for this hour.
Surprise us with the discovery of how much power we have
  to make a difference in our day. . . .

Use this season of celebration to spark new hope
  and stir up our passion for new possibilities.
Make compassion and the spirit of sacrifice
  to be the new mark of affluence of character.
Strengthen us to face reality
and to withstand the rigor of tough times
  in the anticipation of a bright side beyond the struggle.
Inspire, empower, and sustain us
  until we reach the mountaintop,
  and see that future for which our hearts yearn.
This is our fervent and sincere prayer. Amen.

James Alexander Forbes, Jr. (1935–)
Pastor, Riverside Church, New York

For National Holidays*

O Righteous Ruler of the Universe:
We give you thanks for the heritage and hope
    of our own country,
  as people in every place give thanks for their homelands.
When, as a nation, we walk in your way,
  grant us grace to continue in your will.
When, as a people, we fail you,
  correct us, gently yet without compromise.
Enable those who govern us to seek the welfare
  not only of ourselves
  and of all people who share this planet with us
but also the welfare of our children and our children's children,
  that they may share the gifts we treasure,
  that they may dwell in unity and without fear
    from generation to generation.

---

*In the United States: Presidents' Day, Memorial Day, Independence Day, Veterans Day, and such.

Strengthen our resolve to live up to those national ideals
    whose virtues we proclaim
    but whose practice we have not yet achieved.
Teach us justice, kindness, and humility in your presence.
Speedily bring to us and to all of your people
    that peace which is rooted in integrity,
    which flowers forth as wholeness.
For you, O God, are our Peace. Amen.

On Days Honoring Parents or Grandparents

By grace, O Lord, you are our maker,
    and we your daughters and sons.
When our earthly families reflect your love,
    we rejoice and delight to honor
    those whom we call *"mother"*
    ["father," "grandparents"].
We bless you for their sacrificial service to us,
    for all in them that is kind and nurturing.

But when our earthly families fail
    to point us toward divine love,
give us the courage to believe
    that you are not an evil Father
    because a human parent betrayed us
    or offered us a distorted love.

Especially we pray for those
    who find this to be a difficult day
    because their families have failed them,
    because they have sought to have
    children [or grandchildren]
    but can have none,
    because death has snatched from them
    the offspring that they treasured.
Let them see in this no punishment from you.
Cause them to know that you suffer with them;
assure them of your adoption of them
    into your family,
    which comes into being

not by the will of the flesh
nor human desire
but only by your endless faithfulness and love
made known in Jesus Christ. Amen.

At the Beginning of a New School Year

Divine Instructor, source of all truth:
To all who teach give wisdom.
To all who learn give diligence.
Let not the weakness of the flesh
    diminish the power you have given us
to seek for that which is
    true and honorable and just.
Open minds to new meanings
and hearts to new faithfulness,
through Jesus who, in the Temple,
    both taught and learned. Amen.

For Thanksgiving Day

It is always right, O God,
to praise you and to bless your name.
Even if the harvests fail,
even when economies falter,
    still you are our God;
    still you bless us richly.
Help us to see your active hand
    in bounty or in scarcity,
    in pain as well as pleasure.
When we fail to see you at work
    we fall into the sin of ingratitude,
or even suppose that all that we have
    is the work of our own hands,
    the result of our own intelligence and industry.
Forgive us, and save us
    from an existence so self-centered.
Set us free from greedy and grasping hearts.

By your generosity to us,
    teach us to be generous to others,

and thus to give evidence to you
    that we are indeed your thankful people.
This we pray through Jesus Christ,
    your most gracious and enduring gift to us,
for whom be everlasting praise. Amen.

IV. Acts Appropriate to the Occasion

In Times of Distress, Illness, and Death

For the Sick and Those Who Minister to Them

O God:
In your compassion made known in Jesus,
    look with favor upon those
        who are in distress because of illness
            or accident.
To them give hope and patience,
    and the ability to entrust themselves
        to others and to you.

Enable physicians and nurses
and all who assist them
    to use their training and skill
        in the service of your healing love.
Help them to minister to those in need
    with both hands and hearts of mercy.

Reveal the closeness of your presence
    to those who suffer
        and also to all family members and friends
            who care about them
            and work to alleviate
                their discomfort and anxiety.

According to your wisdom and will
restore to full health those who have yet
    much work to do for you on earth.

To those who must endure long-term illness
    or physical incapacity
  give patience and purpose for
    new kinds of service in the world.
Prepare for death those who shall shortly confront it,
  that they may walk through the valley
    without fear of evil,
    with confidence that on the other side
      they will enter fully into your presence,
        where sorrow and sighing are past.

Receive this prayer through Christ
  who came among us that we might have life,
    and have it abundantly. Amen.

In Times of Great Distress Due to Natural Disaster or Humanly Devised Evil

God, our help and our hope in every time of life:
  we bow before you in distress and confusion.
Devastation and death seem to rule your world today.
We know not where to turn, nor even how to pray.

Assure us that you know our thoughts before we think them,
  that you accept
    petitions that have no words,
    prayers that are inarticulate anguish,
    even anger in the face of events we do not understand.
Remind us of your presence with Jesus
  in his hours of agony,
  in the face of abadonment by many whom he trusted,
  in the pain of crucifixion,
  and even in death itself.
Enable us to know that you do not desert us
  but in times of need stand even closer than before.

Comfort those who mourn.
Give hope to those who seem to have lost all hope.
With your healing power, touch any who are injured;
  to all medical and rescue workers

give patient endurance, wisdom, and skill.
As you give us opportunity to serve those in need,
grant also generous spirits
and the wise and efficient use of our abilities
in offering aid.
If today our words of praise are mute,
if today we find it easier to curse than to bless,
point us to the empty tomb,
which lies beyond the cross.
Remind us that it may be Friday now,
but in your Providence Sunday's coming,
and your love will see us through
every darkness,
every doubt,
every desolation.
For you, O God, are our hope and our strength,
an ever present help in time of trouble;
to you we pray through Jesus Christ
who triumphs over all things. Amen.

For Those with Mental Illness

You, O God, are the author of peace,
and in you is neither confusion nor disorder.
In Jesus you showed your compassion to all who
suffered with troubled spirits.
Therefore look mercifully upon those
whose minds are confused,
to whom this world seems a jumble,
or who live in a world that does not exist.
In their times of agitation and anguish,
calm their spirits.
In their times of clarity,
grant them happy memories
and joy to their present lives.
Give wisdom and gentleness to those who
take care of them,
especially to those who knew them in better times
and now feel helpless and anguished.
Grant them all the promise that in the end

you will restore order and peace
within your eternal home.
Through Jesus, the Healer. Amen.

When You Are Seriously Ill

Lord, I need your strength.
I am weak, but you are strong.
I am sick, but you are the source of all healing.
You know how I feel, for you have suffered far more pain
than I will ever know.

Lord, it's hard to wait patiently for you to renew my strength.
Allow me to share the strength of others,
and lean on them while I wait.
Allow me to experience your strengthening presence
and to rest in you.
Enable me to find that strength
which is possible even in weakness.
And should I never be strong again,
give me grace to be content with
weakness,
hardship, and
disease;
for when I am weak,
because of Jesus Christ, then I am strong. Amen.

Neil Weatherhogg (1939–), alt.
Presbyterian pastor

Thanksgiving after Recovery from an Illness

Gracious God and Healer of both body and spirit:
Blessed are you for hearing my prayer,
for bringing me back
from weakness and fear
into renewed strength and confidence.

Thank you for the many who surrounded me
in the time of my illness and recovery:
physicians, technicians, nurses,
and any who assisted them;
family members and friends;

caring sisters and brothers in Christ;
all who made pastoral calls;
all who prayed for me and with me.
For their loving concern and generous care,
blessed be your name.

By the continuing ministry of your Holy Spirit,
teach me how I may best declare my gratitude
by a deeper devotion to you and your way.
Grant that what I endured
may make more tender my own heart
to the needs of others who suffer.
Show me what direction you would have me take
in the life you continue to lend me,
and how I may best serve you and others
with my body healed
and my spirit lifted higher into your presence.

Through this experience remind me continually
that no one escapes death;
and prepare me so that on the day of my final illness
I may enter into your heavenly presence
without fear,
with confident rejoicing.

Receive my gratitude through Jesus Christ,
who heals the sick
and strengthens the faint of heart,
who offers life eternal to all. Amen.

When Your Own Death Seems Imminent

Holy God, my help and my hope:
my time on earth has been limited
since the hour I was born.
But often my life has seemed to extend
so far into the future
that I could not imagine it coming to an end.
Now the end seems near
and suddenly so real.

Give me the grace to face my death with faith,
    knowing that I now walk in the path
        that Jesus himself took
            as he journeyed to the cross.
By his death, help me to go with trust
    to my death.
By his resurrection, grant me assurance
    that beyond death there is new life,
        with unimagined opportunity and joy.

I offer now forgiveness and grace
        to all who have wounded or failed me,
    even as I beg mercy
        from all whom I have injured,
        and most of all from you, O God.

I commend to you my family members,
    my friends, and all who are dear to me.
Grant them strength in the midst of mourning,
    and guidance in the new ways they shall walk
        without me at their side.

Father: Into your hands I give myself.
Lord Jesus: Receive my spirit.
Divine Breath: Breathe into me eternal life.

Do with me as you will,
    for you are my God,
        and I trust you. Amen.

I beg you, good Jesus,
that as you have graciously granted me here on earth
    to enjoy the sweetness of your wisdom and truth,
so at death you will bring me into your presence.
    that I may see the beauty of your face,
    and listen to your voice
        which is the source of all wisdom and truth. Amen.

Bede (673–735)
English monk and historian

For Any Who Watch with Those to Whom Death Draws Near

God of the dark night,
>you were with Jesus praying in the garden,
>you were with Jesus all the way to the cross
>>and through to the resurrection.
Help us to recognize you now,
>as we watch with *[Name]*,
>and wait for what must happen;
help us through any bitterness and despair,
help us accept our distress,
help us to remember that you care for us
>and that in your will is our peace. Amen.
>>>>*A New Zealand Prayer Book, 1989*

When Mourning the Loss of a Friend

>If death my friend and me divide,
>thou dost not, Lord, my sorrow chide,
>>or frown my tears to see;
>restrained from passionate excess,
>thou bidst me mourn in calm distress
>>for them that rest in thee.

>I feel a strong immortal hope,
>which bears my mournful spirit up
>>beneath its mountain load;
>redeemed from death, and grief, and pain,
>I soon will see my friend again
>>within the arms of God.

>Pass a few fleeting moments more
>and death the blessing will restore
>>which death has snatched away;
>for me thou wilt the summons send,
>and give me back my parted friend
>>in that eternal day. Amen.

>>>>*Charles Wesley (1707–1788)*
>>>>*British clergyman and poet*

For the Bereaved

O Living God, you share all our griefs.
 Give a meaning to that which defies our understanding.
 Shine upon our night.
You alone can show us
 that we are not abandoned to chance or fate,
  not even in what seems revolting or senseless to us,
 but that in all things you work for the good
  of those who love you.
Grant that those who mourn may receive your message
 even through their sufferings.
Through their sorrow challenge them
 to discover the help of your mercy,
 and to hope more fervently for your kingdom.
Through their sadness, open them more to your compassion,
 and help them to live in your strength alone.
Reveal your nearness to those who suffer this day.
Surround them with the love that you have
 for your children,
through Jesus Christ our Savior. Amen.

Reformed Church in France, 1963

Concerning the Life and Mission of the Church

For Your Own Congregation

God of multitudes, ruler of the universe:
Look with favor upon Christ's flock in this place.
 Cause our congregation to be
  an effective witness to your love and power.
To this end, banish from us
 pettiness and rivalry,
 speaking ill of one another,
 seeking to serve ourselves rather than you.
Guide the leaders of the congregation, both lay and ordained,
 that in turn they may guide us also into your ways.
Bind us together by your love
 and cause us to know ourselves to be
  a people called out of darkness into your marvelous light.
This we ask through Christ who himself is head of the church.
Amen.

Before a Congregational Business Meeting

O God, to us you have entrusted the task
   of governing this congregation.
Make us faithful in our service.
Keep our hearts centered on your Good News,
   lest we wander off into pursuits of our own.
In our discussions, give us clarity
   and understanding of differing views.
In our voting, give us wisdom and integrity.
For the sake of fulfilling your mission
   cause us to be good stewards of all
   of the resources of talent, time, and money
   at our disposal.
Your will be done,
   through Christ our Leader. Amen.

For the Lay Leadership of the Church

Blessed Jesus, Head of the Body:
To all laity who give leadership to the church
   grant faith and understanding
such that they may guide your people
   with a spirit of gentleness
   and with their eyes fixed upon your glory.
Let them do nothing for personal gain
   or reputation,
but everything to fulfill the mission
   you have set before us.
This we ask for the sake of the world you love.
Amen.

For the Clergy Leadership of the Church

God of grace:
To all clergy who have taken responsibility
   for the care of your church,
   give a love for the people of God
   equal to a love of the Gospel.
Let no discouragement or spiritual weariness
   overtake them

and no temptation be put in their way
   that they cannot resist.
Enable them to trust you
   and to serve you with gladness
   all the days of their lives,
through Jesus Christ our Lord. Amen.

For Those Being Ordained

Steadfast God:
With all who take upon themselves
   the vows and responsibilities of ordination,
share your steadfastness
that they may keep their promises
both faithfully and joyfully.
Grant them patience, persistence, and endurance,
   especially when they are called upon
   to make difficult decisions,
   to provide counsel in the midst of confusion,
   to stand up for righteous causes
      that are unpopular in their communities.
Make them good shepherds under him
   who is Chief Shepherd of the flock,
   Jesus our redeemer. Amen.

For Bishops and Other Leaders of the Church

Good Shepherd, chief leader of your flock:
   Give to those who serve in authority under you
      your concern for the sheep,
      your protection of the sheep, and
      your attention to the sheep.
Direct particularly the hearts of the bishops,*
   that they may fulfill their calling
      to teach the people and
      to guard the church from error.
When the burden of their task grows heavy,

---

*Various denominations use differing titles for the administrative leaders of the church. Adapt the language here to fit your situation.

remind them that you are their help and strength.
When perplexity is about to overwhelm them,
   cause them to discern what is
      your perfect will for the church
      and for the world which the church is called to serve.
Let them by their gentleness
   reveal you more fully.
For it is in you, with you, and through you that we pray. Amen.

For the Legislative Bodies of the Church

In The United Methodist Church, the basic regional legislative body, the Annual Conference, meets each year, usually in the late spring.

Every four years, The General Conference, the denominational legislative body, meets in April and/or May of presidential election years in the U.S.A. This is the supreme policy-making body of The United Methodist Church.

In July of those same years, five United Methodist geographical units within the United States meet to elect bishops and conduct other regional business. These are known as Jurisdictional Conferences.

The following prayer is adapatable for all such sessions.

Those who belong to other denominations will need to alter the prayer where italicized words appear in order to fit their systems of church government, which may use the term "Diocese," "Presbytery," "General Assembly," "Synod," and so on, rather than the term "Conference."

You have called us, O God,
   to do the work of your church
      as careful and efficient stewards.
To this end we bind together our congregations
   and govern them through the work
      of *Conferences* in which we consult
      and consider together
      pressing matters before the church.
Give wisdom and vision to those who serve us
   as delegates to our

Annual/Jurisdictional/General Conference, etc.
Let not the weariness of their duties distract them
nor the emotion of the issues they face prejudice them
    in the decisions they must make.

Enable them to seek first your kingdom and its righteousness.

For use by United Methodists only in years when Jurisdictional Conferences meet:
So also instruct in your ways
    our delegates to the Jurisdictional Conferences,
that they may wisely elect the bishops of our church
    and conduct other necessary business before them.

For use in all instances:
Give all delegates a love for your whole church—
    a desire not only to serve you as we now can
    but also a determination to bring unity
        to divided churches,
that the world may more readily receive the Gospel
    and find in our manner of living it out
        the way of peace and unity.
Through Christ who is the head of the body, the church. Amen.

For the Courts of the Church

O God, the righteous Judge of all the earth:
Give your wisdom and counsel
    to those who are called upon
        to determine the guilt or innocence of church officials
            who stand accused,
    and to those whose reponsibility it is
        to interpret the laws of our church.

Especially we pray for the members of
    The Judicial Council of The United Methodist Church;*
grant them the gifts of fairness and sound understanding
    that the church may be an example before the world
        of your justice and mercy;
through Jesus Christ our Savior. Amen.

---

*Here may be substituted titles of church courts within your denomination.

For the Unity of the Church Universal

Most blessed and glorious Trinity,
three persons in One God:
Teach us to worship and adore thee.

And that we may adore thee,
    that our worship may not be a mockery,
make us to know that we are one in Christ,
        as the Father is one with the Son,
        as the Son is one with the Father.
Forbid us to look upon sectarianism
    as if it were a destiny.
Help us to regard it as rebellion against thee.
Help us to see all distinctions more clearly
    in the light of thy everlasting love.
Help us to recognize the truth of every effort
    to express something of that which passes knowledge.
Help us to feel and confess the feebleness of our own efforts.

So may thy holy name embrace us more and more.
So may all creatures in heaven and earth
    at last glorify thee throughout all ages. Amen.
                    Frederick Denison Maurice (1805–1872), alt.
                    English theologian and social reformer

For a Just and Compassionate Society

For God's Help in Alleviating Injustice

To thee, O Lord, we make our plea
that human sorrows thou wouldst see,
and human grief, and human tears
that flow throughout the life-long years.

Awake, O Lord, and speak the word;
awake, assert thyself as Lord.
And let the pain of head and heart
at thy dear coming, Lord, depart.

Awake and let thy people know
that from them thou wilt never go;
and let the world be put to shame
if, Lord, it reverence not thy name. Amen.

Benjamin Tucker Tanner (1835–1923)
AME bishop and father of artist,
Henry Osawa Tanner

The above text may be sung to the following familiar tunes:
GERMANY ("Where Cross the Crowded Ways of Life")
HAMBURG ("When I Survey the Wondrous Cross")
MARYTON ("O Master, Let Me Walk with Thee")

For Freedom from Racial Prejudice

O God, thou hast made us in thine own image,
and thou dost love all whom thou hast made.
Suffer us not because of difference of race, color, or condition
to separate ourselves from others
and thereby from thee;
but teach us the unity of thy family
and the universality of thy love.

As thou, Savior, as a Son, was born of a Hebrew mother
(who had the blood of many nations in her veins)
and ministered first to thy brethren of the Israelites,
but rejoiced in the faith
of a Syro-Phoenecian woman
and of a Roman soldier,
and suffered thy cross to be carried by an Ethiopian:

Teach us also, while loving and serving our own,
to enter into the communion of the whole family;
and forbid that
from pride of birth, color, achievement
and from hardness of heart
we should despise any for whom Christ died,
or injure or grieve any in whom he lives.
We pray in Jesus' precious name. Amen.

Robert C. Lawson (1883–1961)
Pentecostal pastor and bishop

For Those Who Know the Sting of Discrimination

Tender God, just and compassionate:
Extend your consolation and strength
  to all of those bear ridicule, isolation, and even persecution
    from those who find fault where there is none,
    from those who place blame in matters over which
     · the ones they blame have no control.
To all who know this sting
  give the assurance that you stand near to them,
    that in your love is their hope
    and their release from guilt and shame and fear.
Grant that we who pray for them
  may also struggle valiantly
    to assist them in all ways open to us,
    to alleviate the causes of their distress,
    to cry out against discrimination everywhere.

Enable us to recall any pain we ourselves have felt
    because others belittled or rejected us,
  so that our concern may be genuine;
enable us to recall any pain we have caused others
    by judging and excluding them,
  so that our concern may be free from self-righteousness.
This we pray in the name of Jesus,
  who was scorned because he came from Nazareth. Amen.

To Be Led in the Ways of Justice and Peace

O God, ruler of righteousness,
  lead us, we pray, in the ways of justice and peace.
Inspire us to break down all oppression and wrong,
  to gain for everyone their own due reward,
    and from everyone their due service,
  that each may live for all,
  and all may live for each,
in the name of Jesus Christ our Lord. Amen.

William Temple (1881–1944), alt.
Archbishop of Canterbury

For Justice in Our Communities and the World

Almighty God,
who hast created us in thine own image:
Grant us grace fearlessly
   to contend against evil, and
   to make no peace with oppression;
and, that we may reverently use our freedom,
help us to employ it in the maintenance of justice
   in our communities and among the nations,
   to the glory of thy holy name;
through Jesus Christ our Lord,
who lives and reigns with thee and the Holy Spirit,
   one God, now and forever. Amen.

James Martineau (1805–1900)
British pastor and scholar

For the Future

Gracious God,
   let your will for us all be known.
   Let all be partners in shaping the future
     with a faith that quarrels with the present
      for the sake of what yet might be. Amen.

Anonymous, from Taiwan

In the Struggle for Truth

God,
   whose name defies definition,
   but whose will is known in freeing the oppressed,
make us to be one with all who cry for justice,
   that we who speak your praise may struggle for your truth;
through Jesus Christ. Amen.

Janet Morley
Advocate for the ordination of women
in the Church of England

For Those Who Grow Weary in the Struggle for Justice

God, righteous and enduring:
Look with pity upon those
  who grow weary and discouraged in their work for justice.
When it seems to them
  that nothing ever changes for the better,
  that the forces of evil will always prevail,
remind them that you, the Almighty, have endured
  not years or decades of resistance,
  but whole centuries and indeed millennia.
Yet you promise that your righteousness will triumph,
  that evil will collapse.

Save the tired strivers after justice from the doom of Sisyphus:
  daily hoisting a mighty rock up a high hill,
    only to have it tumble down again.
Assure them
  that the stones they move,
    by grace will be assembled into a house of righteousness
    upon the highest of the mountains,
  and that all the peoples of the earth shall stream to it,
    that all may walk in the ways of the Lord.

Grant this through Jesus, the chief foundation stone. Amen.

Prayers for Times of the Day

Morning

Lord Jesus Christ,
you are the sun that always rises but never sets.
You are the source of all life,
    creating and sustaining every living thing.
You are the source of all food, material and spiritual,
    nourishing us in both body and soul.
You are the light that dispels the clouds of error and doubt,
    and goes before me every hour of the day,
        guiding my thoughts and actions.
May I walk in your light,
be sustained by your mercy,
and be warmed by your love. Amen.

Erasmus (1469–1536)
Renowned Dutch scholar and church reformer

God of the morning, at whose voice
    the cheerful sun makes haste to rise,
and like a giant doth rejoice
    to run his journies through the skies:
O, like the sun, may I fulfill
    the appointed duties of the day.
with ready mind and active will
    march on and keep my heavenly way. Amen.

Isaac Watts (1674–1748)
English poet and clergyman

Midday

God, ever present:
Refresh me as I pause in the midst of my daily routine.

I pause to remember that already you have been
        at work in my life this day,
    whether I have noticed it or not,
    whether I have remembered to give thanks for it or not.

Grant that I may live this whole day to your honor and glory
 as a faithful disciple of Jesus Christ. Amen.

Evening

When the day returns call us up
  with morning faces and with morning hearts,
    eager to labor,
  happy, if happiness be our portion,
  and if the day be marked for sorrow, strong to endure.
  Amen.

Robert Louis Stevenson (1850–1894)
British author

Be among us, O merciful God, and protect us
  through the silent hours of this night.
Grant that we, who are wearied by
  the changes and the chances of this fleeting world,
may rest upon your eternal changelessness;
through Jesus Christ our Lord.

Traditional prayer for Compline

Other Resources

A Centering Prayer

Whenever you pray, go into your room and shut the door. (Matthew 6:6)
  Lord, I have shut the door, speak now the word
  which in the din and throng could not be heard.
    Hush now my inner heart, whisper thy will,
    while I have come apart, while all is still.

In this blest quietness clamorings cease;
here in thy presence dwells infinite peace.
  Yonder, the strife and cry, yonder, the sin:
  Lord, I have shut the door; thou art within.

Lord, I have shut the door; strengthen my heart.
Yonder awaits the task—I share a part.

Only through grace bestowed may I be true.
Here, while alone with thee, my strength renew. Amen.

William M. Runyan (1870–1957)
Composer and hymn text writer

The prayer above may be sung to the tune commonly used with the text "Break Thou the Bread of Life, Dear Lord to Me."

A Prayer to the Holy Spirit

Holy Spirit, the life that gives life:
you are the cause of all movement;
you are the breath of all creatures;
you are the salve that purifies our souls;
you are the ointment that heals our wounds;
you are the fire that warms our hearts;
you are the light that guides our feet.
Let all the world praise you. Amen.

Hildegard of Bingen (1098–1179)
German nun and mystic

Before Reading the Scriptures

Lord, as I read the Psalms
    let me hear you singing.
As I read your words,
    let me hear you speaking.
As I reflect on each page,
    let me see your image.
And as I seek to put your precepts into practice,
    let my heart be filled with joy. Amen.

Lady Jane Grey (1537–1554)
British monarch, deposed by Mary Tudor after nine days

Discipleship

Almighty, eternal, just and merciful God:
    Grant us the desire to do only what pleases you,
    and the strength to do only what you command.
Cleanse our souls,
enlighten our minds,

and inflame our hearts with your Holy Spirit,
that we may follow in the footsteps of your beloved Son,
Jesus Christ. Amen.

St. Francis of Assisi (1182–1226)
Italian monk and reformer of the church

Divine Love

Dear Lord:
It seems you are so madly in love with your creatures
that you could not live without us.
So you created us;
and then, when we turned away from you, you redeemed us.
Yet you are God, and so have no need of us.
Your greatness is made no greater by our creation;
your power is made no stronger by our redemption.
You have no duty to care for us, no debt to repay us.
It is love, and love alone, that moves you. Amen.

Catherine of Siena (c. 1347–1380)
Italian nun and mystic

For Spiritual Concentration

God, help my thoughts!
They stray from me,
setting off on the wildest journeys.
When I am in church,
they run off like naughty children,
quarreling and making trouble.
When I read the Bible,
they fly to a distant city,
filled with temptations.

My thoughts can cross an ocean with a single leap.
They can fly from earth to heaven and back again,
in a single second.
They come to me for a fleeting moment,
and then away they flee.
No chains, no locks can hold them back.
No threats of punishment can restrain them.

No hiss of a lash can frighten them.
They slip from my grasp like tails of eels.
They swoop hither and thither like swallows in flight.

Dear holy Christ, who can see into every heart
    and read every mind:
Take hold of my thoughts.
Bring my thoughts back to me,
    and clasp me to yourself. Amen.

Celtic prayer

A Student's Prayer

O Lord, you are the fountain of all wisdom and learning.
You have given me the years of my youth
    to learn the arts and skills necessary
        to live an honest and holy life.
Enlighten my mind, that I may acquire knowledge.
Strengthen my memory that I may retain what I have learned.
Govern my heart, that I may always be
    eager and diligent in all of my studies.
And cause your Spirit of truth, judgment, and prudence
    to guide my understanding,
that I may perceive how everything I learn
    fits into your holy plan for the world. Amen.

John Calvin (1509–1564)
Reformation leader and theologian

The Lord's Prayer: Current Ecumenical Text

Our Father in heaven,
    hallowed be your name,
    your kingdom come,
    your will be done, on earth as in heaven.
Give us today our daily bread.
Forgive us our sins
    as we forgive those who sin agaist us.
Save us from the time of trial
    and deliver us from evil.
For the kingdom, the power, and the glory are yours
        now and for ever. Amen.

The Lord's Prayer: A Traditional Text

Our Father, who art in heaven,
    hallowed be thy name.
Thy kingdom come,
    thy will be done on earth as it is in heaven.
Give us this day our daily bread.
And forgive us our trespasses,
    as we forgive those who trespass against us.
And lead us not into temptation,
    but deliver us from evil.
For thine is the kingdom, and the power, and the glory,
    forever. Amen.

The Lord's Prayer: Another Traditional Text

Our Father, who art in heaven,
    hallowed be thy name;
    thy kingdom come,
    thy will be done, on earth as it is in heaven.
Give us this day our daily bread;
and forgive us our debts,
    as we forgive our debtors;
and lead us not into temptation,
    but deliver us from evil.
For thine is the kingdom and the power and the glory,
    forever. Amen.

The Apostles' Creed

I believe in God the Father Almighty,
        maker of heaven and earth.

And in Jesus Christ his only Son our Lord:
    who was conceived by the Holy Spirit,
        born of the Virgin Mary,
        suffered under Pontius Pilate,
        was crucified, dead, and buried;
    the third day he rose from the dead;
    he ascended into heaven,
        and sitteth at the right hand of God the Father Almighty;
    from thence he shall come to judge the living and the dead.
I believe in the Holy Spirit,
        the holy catholic church,

the communion of saints,
the forgiveness of sins,
the resurrection of the body,
and the life everlasting. Amen.

The Nicene Creed

We believe in one God,
the Father, the Almighty,
maker of heaven and earth,
of all that is, seen and unseen.

We believe in one Lord, Jesus Christ,
the only Son of God,
eternally begotten of the Father,
God from God, Light from Light,
true God from true God,
begotten, not made,
of one Being with the Father;
through him all things were made.
For us and for our salvation
he came down from heaven,
was incarnate of the Holy Spirit and the Virgin Mary
and became truly human.
For our sake he was crucified under Pontius Pilate;
he suffered death and was buried.
On the third day he rose again
in accordance with the Scriptures;
he ascended into heaven
and is seated at the right hand of the Father.
He will come again in glory
to judge the living and the dead,
and his kingdom will have no end.

We believe in the Holy Spirit, the Lord, the giver of life,
who proceeds from the Father and the Son,
who with the Father and the Son
is worshiped and glorified,
who has spoken through the prophets.
We believe in the one holy catholic and apostolic church.
We acknowledge one baptism
for the forgiveness of sins.
We look for the resurrection of the dead,
and the life of the world to come. Amen.

V. Personal Prayer Surrounding the Congregational Service

The service of the congregation is greatly aided by the personal prayers of those who comprise it. The Lord's Day Service is not intended to be a monologue to which the congregation listens passively but rather an active dialogue between the people and God.

The suggestions below for facilitating such a dialogue follow a commonly accepted Sunday order of major denominations; if the order used by your congregation differs, you will need to rearrange the sequence of some of the prayers and responses.

Since these prayers are largely to be offered silently and without consulting a book, it will be necessary to commit to memory at least the basic content of each prayer or response, if not the actual words. Therefore do not attempt to memorize all of these at once, but learn them gradually, over a period of months or even a year or longer. Concentrate on mastering one before going on to learn another.

Prayer at the Beginning of The Lord's Day

This may be used upon arising on Sunday morning; or you may prefer to follow the biblical practice of beginning the day of worship at sunset on Saturday evening. In either case, say silently:
This is the day which the Lord has made.
We will rejoice and be glad in it.
On this day the church perpetually remembers
the resurrection of Jesus from the dead.
In this death and resurrection we find life.

Preparation of the Sunday Offering

It is commendable to have a brief time on Saturday evening or Sunday morning to set aside the money or write out the check for the day's offering. At the end of 1 Corinthians Paul gave an extended and exalted consideration to the nature of the resurrection and then gave instructions to the church "concerning the collection ... on the first day of every week" (1 Cor. 15:1–16:4). This sequence in the thought of the apostle encourages us to see the offering not as a necessity, so that the church may pay its bills, but as a tangible way of giving thanks for the hope we are offered in the resurrection. As you prepare your offering, say silently:

Grant me, O Lord, such gratitude for your glorious resurrection
that I may give this offering cheerfully.
Increase my generosity toward others more and more,
as one sign of my love for you. Amen.

Upon Departing for the Congregational Service

Where distance and physical conditions make it possible, it is commendable to walk to the place of worship, for walking can be a time for quiet reflection and prayer. In any event, as you approach the church building say silently Psalm 122:1:

I was glad when they said to me,
    "Let us go to the house of the LORD!"

Upon Greeting Fellow Worshipers

When greeting fellow worshipers before being seated for the service, say silently or aloud:

The peace of the Lord be with you.

During Silence or Instrumental Music

Once at your seat, pray
    for your fellow worshipers, by name if possible, that you and they may
        present a sacrifice of praise and thanksgiving acceptable to God;
    for any you know to be absent for good cause, that God may work

within them, as within you, and that they may soon return
to the weekly assembly of the faithful;
for all who are absent without cause, that their faith may be rekindled,
and that by their presence the assembly of the faithful may be
enhanced;
for any, present or absent, with whom you have had
misunderstandings,
or from whom you feel alienated, that the peace of the church may be
restored through God's reconciling love.
As time allows, pray also for spiritual concentration throughout the
service and for more fruitful service to God as a result of the service.

As Music Is to Be Sung Throughout the Service

As a hymn tune is played before the hymn is sung, pray silently
Psalm 149:1 or Psalm 150:6:
Sing praise in the assembly of the faithful.
Let everything that breathes praise the LORD.

After an Anthem or Solo

At the conclusion of music sung by a choir or soloist, pray silently:
Accept this music, offered up on behalf of us all,
and to you alone be the glory, O God. Amen.

At the Reading of the Scriptures

Unless your congregation uses a spoken prayer or response at this
point, as the Scriptures are about to be read, pray silently:
O Lord, open my ears and my heart to your Word. Amen.

After the Sermon

Unless there is a spoken prayer after the sermon, pray silently:
What I have heard with the ear,
give me grace to do in my life. Amen.

At the Creed

Just before the creed is said, remembering Romans 10:9, pray silently:
Enable me to profess with my lips
and to believe in my heart that Jesus is Lord. Amen.

At the conclusion of the creed, pray silently:
Grant that I may live and die in the faith of
your one holy catholic and apostolic church. Amen.

After the Prayers of the People

After the thanksgivings and intercessions, pray silently:
Enable me, good Lord, to remember in my prayers this week
those for whom we have prayed this morning,
and all who are in any need. Amen.

At the Commitment of Others

When persons are to be baptized and received into membership, or wish to commit themselves to a particular kind of discipleship, as they present themselves pray silently:
Grant that what they promise, holy God,
they may do without fail,
by the strength of your grace. Amen.

After these persons have completed their acts of commitment, pray silently:
Give us grace as a congregation to support these faithfully
with our prayers and encouragement,
that they and we may
keep the promises made this day. Amen.

At the Offering

As the offering is being received pray:
that all may give generously, according to their ability;

that all may give cheerfully, not out of duty but for the joy of it;
that the church may carefully and wisely
use the money entrusted to it,
   not for its own needs alone but for the welfare of others,
   and particularly for the poor,
      that they may know the joy of the Lord
      and the graciousness of the people of God.

Before the Sacrament of the Lord's Supper

As the Table is made ready, and before the Great Thanksgiving begins,
say silently:
   As we, your people, come to this, your table,
   refresh and strengthen us for greater service to you. Amen.

Throughout the Great Thanksgiving, say or sing boldly all of the
words prescribed for congregational use.

As you receive the bread and cup say silently or aloud:
   Thanks be to God.
   and/or
   Amen.

   While at your pew, as others receive before or after you, pray for
them and for their particular needs, that they may be effective witnesses
to the power and grace of God because they have been strengthened
inwardly with this sacramental gift.

At the Blessing and Dismissal

If no unison response is provided, after the blessing say silently:
   Thanks be to God, whose blessing sustains us.

At the Departure

As you leave the building to return home, say Psalm 84:1, 10 silently:
   How lovely is your dwelling place,

O L<small>ORD</small> of hosts!
I would rather be a doorkeeper in the house of my God
than live in the tents of wickedness.

Personal Prayer When Participation in the Service of the Congregation Is Not Possible

Illness, travel, conflicting work schedules, and a variety of other causes on occasion will prevent you from being present with the congregation on the Lord's Day. But this need not prevent you from praying with and for them. When possible, engage in such prayer at the same hour as congregational worship is being held.

You may use the order for this day of the month as a framework for your personal prayer. But within that daily order give particular attention to the following:

- Pray for all who attend the congregational service, that they may render to God an acceptable sacrifice of praise and thanksgiving.
- Pray particularly for musicians who lead the service, and for those who read the Scriptures aloud or preach, that their ministries may be of benefit to God's people.
- If Holy Communion is celebrated today and the elements from the Lord's Table are to be brought to you, pray that you may be a faithful recipient of this gift; ask that by means of the reception from the common Table you may be united to the congregation, though absent from them in body.
- Pray that by God's will you may be able again to join with the congregation in Sunday services, or if this not be the will of the Lord that you may be united in spirit both to Christ and to his worshiping community of faith.

VI. Use of the Psalms in Times of Trouble and Terror

Within the thirty-one daily orders in this book, psalm portions are selected to serve as acts of praise and thanksgiving to God. But the one hundred fifty psalms contain many other kinds of materials, some of which many devout people have deemed unsuitable for Christians.

There are sentiments of complaint to God: "Remove your stroke from me; I am worn down by the blows of your hands" (Ps. 39:10). "I sink in deep mire, where there is no foothold; I have come into deep waters, and the flood sweeps over me. I am weary with my crying; my throat is parched. My eyes grow dim with waiting for my God" (69:2-3).

There are vile curses on the enemies of the psalmist: "Let them be put to shame and dishonor who seek after my life. Let them be turned back and confounded who devise evil against me. Let them be like chaff before the wind, with the angel of the LORD driving them" (35:4-5). "O God, break the teeth in their mouths.... Let them vanish like water that runs away; like grass let them be trodden down and wither. Let them be like the snail that dissolves into slime; like the untimely birth that never sees the sun" (58:6-8).

Most notorious in this regard is Psalm 137. It begins so beautifully as a lament by the Jews exiled in Babylon: "By the rivers of Babylon—there we sat down and wept when we remembered Zion.... How could we sing the Lord's song in a foreign land?" But then it turns vengeful and ends thus: "O daughter of Babylon, you devastator! Happy shall they be who pay you back what you have done to us. Happy shall they be who take your little ones and dash them against the rock!" End of psalm!

Certainly it is not a Christian sentiment to want the babies of the enemy thrown against the rocks. That does not square with Jesus' talk about loving your enemies, going the second mile, turning the other cheek, and such. But if we are deeply honest, must we not confess that often in our hearts we harbor and even nurture sub-Christian sentiments? How many of us on September 11, 2001, smiled benignly into our television sets and said sweetly: "God loves those terrorists, and we love them, too." No! In our hearts we were quite ready to see their babies dashed against the rocks. Pretending that our thoughts are more noble than those of the psalmist is at times sheer self-delusion.

Which do you suppose God prefers from us: Dishonest words which cloak our inner anger or straightforward admission of uncharitable thoughts that God knows from afar, even before the words are on our lips? It is impossible to lie to God.

Furthermore, directing our anger at God is far less damaging than taking it out on whoever it is we happen to dislike at the moment. If we can go into the prayer closet, shut the door, and spew out our venom on the Almighty (who can both accept it and transform it), is that not better than taking it out on a spouse, our children, neighbors who annoy us, or people half a world away whom we have never met but have the capacity of bombing to extinction if we put our national mind to it?

To neglect the psalms we deem less than Christian may greatly diminish our own growth in grace. The ancient church knew that, or it would have removed much of the Psalter from its Scriptures. Instead, it gave the entire Book of Psalms a very honored place. In some traditions that have multiple daily services (such as monasteries), all one hundred fifty psalms are said or sung each week, and in other traditions the entire Psalter is used each month. Still other churches use at least one psalm in Sunday worship each week. In all of these settings, it is understood that not everything in the Psalter is noble. Even then, that at which we cringe tells us who we are at our worst and leads us, if not to songs of exaltation, to prayers of confession.

Finally, the hatred of evil that is evident in the Psalms says to us that God's love of justice and God's determination to exterminate injustice must be taken seriously; otherwise we surrender the hope of a new heaven and a new earth. The esteemed Christian writer C. S. Lewis put it well:

These old poets were, in a sense, near to God. Though hideously distorted by the human instrument, something of the Divine voice can be heard in these passages. Not, of course, that God looks upon their enemies as they do.... But doubtless [God] has for the sin of those enemies just the implacable hostility which the poets express. Implacable? Yes, not to the sinner but to the sin. It will not be tolerated nor condoned, no treaty will be made with it....

The ferocious parts of the Psalms serve as a reminder that there is in the world such a thing as wickedness and that it (if not its perpetrators) is hateful to God. In that way, however dangerous the human distortion may be, [God's] word sounds through these passages too. (*Reflections on the Psalms*, [New York: Harcourt Brace Jovanovich, 1958], 32-33)

Therefore, here are psalms to which you may wish to turn for private use on the occasions specified:

During severe personal illness
    6:1-7, 22, 38, 41
In times of personal depression
    42
When God seems distant or uncaring about wrong
    10, 13, 17
When you are envious of the apparent success of others
    49, 62, 73
When you have sinned greatly
    51
When misunderstood or under attack by others
    5, 7, 28, 31, 35, 37, 69
In times of national/international distress
    53, 57, 60
In times of personal distress
    25

Ultimately, the use of the psalms that seem distasteful will enable you to create your own laments, suitable to distressing occasions in life. Here follow two such prayers based on particular psalms but adopted for contemporary use.

A Responsive Psalm Used after 9/11

Biblical Psalms	Contemporary Adaptations

Hear my prayer, O LORD;
    give ear ... in your faithfulness;
    answer me in your
    righteousness.
	Hear our prayer, O Lord,
	    for you are faithful and
	    righteous.

Do not enter into judgment with
    your servant....
	**We cry to you: do not judge
	    us,**

For the enemy has pursued me, crushing my life to the ground....	**for we have been crushed.**

I remember the days of old,	We remember the days of old,
	    when our cities were secure,
	    our future assured.

I think about all your deeds.
I meditate on the works of
    your hands.
	**We recall all the wonders
	    you have done;
	we celebrate the work of
	    your hands.**

I stretch out my hands to you;
    my soul thirsts for you like a
    parched land.
	We reach out to you;
	we thirst for you like a
	    parched land.

Answer me quickly, O LORD;
    my spirit fails.
	**Answer us quickly, O Lord;
	    our spirit fails.**

Do not hide your face from me,
    or I shall be like those
        who go down to the Pit.
	Do not hide your face from us,
	    or we shall be like those
	        who live with death.

Let me hear of your
    steadfast love
        in the morning,
    for in you I put my trust.
	**Let us hear of your
	    steadfast love
	        in the morning,
	    for in you we put our trust.**

Teach me the way I should
    go,
    for to you I lift up my soul.
	Teach us the way we should
	    go,
	    for we offer you ourselves.

Save me, O LORD, from my
    enemies;
I have fled to you for refuge.
	**Save us from our enemies
	    and forgive our sins;
	    for you are our refuge.**

Teach me to do your will,
    for you are my God.
	Teach us to do your will,
	    for you are our God.

Let your good spirit lead me
   on a level path.
For your name's sake....
      Psalm 143:1-11

Let your good spirit lead us
   on a level path,
for the glory of your name.

Let your compassion come
   speedily to meet us,
for we are brought very low.
Help us, O God of our
   salvation,
   for the glory of your name.
      Psalm 79:8b, 9a

Send us your love speedily
   to welcome us,
for we are brought very low.
Help us, O God of our
   salvation,
   for the glory of your name.

For your name's sake, O LORD,
preserve my life.
In your righteousness bring me
   out of trouble.
      Psalm 143:11

Lord, preserve our life,

bring us out of trouble
   for your name's sake.

Do not remember against us the
   iniquities of our ancestors....

Do not remember the sins
   of our ancestors,
for we are your servants.

Then we your people,
   the flock of your pasture,
will give thanks to you forever;

And we, your own people,
   the flock of your pasture,
will give you unending
   thanks.

from generation to generation

From generation to
   generation

will we recount your praise.
      Psalm 79:8a, 13

  we will sing your praise.
Amen.
      Blair Gilmer Meeks

Here is a much more personal lament, an adaptation of Psalm 55, such as might give expression to the anguish of a business owner whose trusted partner has suddenly left to form a competing corporation. This partner has taken along all mailing lists of clients as well as secrets of the success of the operation, and has recruited current employees to work for the new firm. Faced with anger and anguish, the betrayed partner adapts portions of Psalm 55 as a personal prayer:

Psalm 55

Give ear to my prayer, O God;
do not hide yourself from my
    supplication.
Attend to me, and answer me;
I am troubled in my complaint.

I am distraught by the noise of
    the enemy....the terrors of
    death have fallen upon me.
Fear and trembling come upon me,
and horror overwhelms me.

verses 1-5

My companion laid hands on a
    friend
and violated a covenant with me,

with speech smoother than butter,

but with a heart set on war;
with words that were softer than
    oil.

verses 20-21

It is not enemies who taunt me—

I could bear that;
it is not adversaries who deal
    insolently with me. . . .

But it is you, my equal,
    my companion, my familiar
    friend.

verses 12-13

Personal Lament

Receive my prayer, O God,
and do not hide yourself
    from my anguish.
Answer me,
for I am troubled and
    distraught.

Terrors have fallen upon me,

and trembling comes over me.
I do not know if I can
    endure.

For the one I trusted

has violated a covenant
    with me,
with speech smoother than
    butter,

with words softer than oil,
taking in those who worked
    beside me
and making them my
    enemies.

It is not my old competitors
    who taunt me—
I could bear that.
It is not adversaries who deal
    insolently with me,
but those whom I trusted,
those with whom I have
    shared happy times.

It is my equals, my
companions, my friends

who have risen up against
me.
For envy and greed have
become their friends.

Evening and morning and at
noon
I utter my complaint and moan.
verse 17

Horror overwhelms me.
verse 5b

Let death come upon them.
verse 15a

Confuse, O Lord, confound their
speech.
verse 9
God ... will hear, and will humble
them.
verse 19

But I will trust in you.
verse 23c

Evening, morning, and at
noon
I utter my complaint and
moan.
What shall become of me?
Horror overwhelms me.

Let disaster come upon
them, O God.

Confound their plans and
humble them.

For in you do I trust,
and you will save me.
Accept me for the sake of
Jesus Christ,
and sustain me with your
goodness.
Amen.

Granted, this is another of those prayers that may be dis-
missed as "sub-Christian." But these are the thoughts of the
heart of the betrayed businessowner; and God knows these
thoughts whether they are concealed or confessed. Nothing is
gained by seeking to deceive God. And perhaps the virtues of
the gospel cannot enter the petitioner's heart until these unworthy sentiments are evacuated to make room for that which is
honorable and gracious. Surely the God who brought light out

of darkness at creation can also bring light into the dark recesses of our hearts—if only we will open our hearts to our Maker through honest prayer. It is precisely this which the psalms of ancient Israel teach us how to do.

So let the psalmist be your tutor in the school of prayer.

VII. Teaching Children to Pray

Children learn best how to talk to God in the same way that they learn to talk to people—by overhearing the conversation of adults. Children are born mimics and will readily copy what they observe others doing.

We do not expect our children to learn to talk by telling them, "Every sentence needs at least a noun or pronoun and a verb. Often the verb takes an object, usually another noun." We may teach children such rules of language in school, but that is years after they have begun to speak. Then rules of grammar function as a form of analysis, not as a source of initial learning. Recent studies in the psychology of children indicate that infants are overhearing and beginning to understand their native language many months before they are capable of articulating words.

Therefore, let children overhear prayer at church and in the home. From early childhood I was carried to a small one-room church that had no separate "nursery." I am not convinced of the appropriateness of removing children from the midst of the worshiping congregation. This separation exists largely for the comfort and convenience of the adults, and we need to ask whether children gain more or lose more in the process. Where church nurseries are popular (and where aren't they?), can the children be brought into the worshiping assembly at least to witness baptisms, to receive communion, and to hear the liturgies of Christmas Eve and Easter morning?

Surely this much is beyond dispute: The fewer the occasions on which young children are in the midst of the praying congregation, the greater the need for family prayer at home, where the children may overhear and thus come to imitate ways of talking to God. The demise of family prayer together with the growth of

173

nursery facilities during the congregational service leaves our children ignorant of any prayer except that which is self-centered and self-serving. The restoration of family prayer with children present is urgent.

When a child is old enough to begin to do more than eavesdrop on the prayers of others, it is well for adults in the family first to offer prayers on behalf of the child and only later to expect that child to make prayer on his or her own. Parents and grandparents will need to assess carefully when these steps are best taken for each child. Just as some children begin to speak very early and others cause their parents to fear that they will be mute into adulthood, so there is no "magic moment" at which every child can be expected to frame a prayer.

At first the content of prayers said by children or on their behalf needs to be simple and concrete. Prayers for world peace and justice, for example, must eventually be introduced, but in early childhood these abstract concepts are sources of mystification rather than edification. The content most readily accessible to the very young can be categorized as "The Three F's"—food, family, friends.

Adults can start with food by regularly praying at mealtimes and allowing the very young to overhear. The etiquette of respectful silence while prayer is being offered can be taught: "Now we are going to be quiet, and mother will talk to God for all of us." Where it is the custom to bow the head, close the eyes, and fold the hands, these can be taught. Table graces are normally brief and this fits nicely with the limited attention span of children.

As the child develops, prayers at bedtime can be introduced, including intercessions for family members and friends. At first, this will mean persons the child knows well. Over time, care should be taken to introduce the child to the idea that God's family is larger than our birth families, and that God is the supreme Friend of us all. Here we move from concretion to abstraction, and that is tricky with children. It is well for us to give them concepts that they can grow into over time. The fact that children have no idea what it means to say "The Lord is my shepherd" should not prevent us from teaching them Psalm 23 while their memories are uncluttered, even if it takes them decades or a whole lifetime to grasp the rich realities of such metaphorical speech.

In moving from prayers children overhear adults say to prayers that even children utter on their own behalf, there is a crucial intermediate step that can be called "guided prayer." It may best occur as the closing event of family prayer just before the child's bedtime, and it can arise out of a simple review of the child's activities that day:

Adult: What happened today that made you happy?

Child: We had fun playing outside this afternoon.

Adult: Then let's thank God in this way: "God, thank you for the warm weather, for the green grass, for times of laughing and having fun. Thank you for the friends and playmates you give."

[Once the child becomes familiar with the procedure, the child may be encouraged to speak the prayer phrase-by-phrase after the adult.]

Adult: What happened today that made you unhappy?

Child: It rained this evening when we were supposed to go swimming.

Adult: Then let's talk to God in this way: "Sometimes we do not get to do what we wanted to do. But the flowers and the vegetables in our gardens need rain to grow. O God, help us to understand that at times what we want to do may not be the best thing for all."

Adult: Did you do anything today for which you are sorry?

Child: I should not have hit my sister when we were fighting over toys.

Adult: Let's tell God that. "Dear God, sometimes I am unkind to others. I am sorry for being mean. Help me to be more kind."

Adult: Whom do you love and care about, who needs God's help?

Child: Timmy is in the hospital and is very sick.

Adult: Let's pray for Timmy and those who help to make him better: "Watch over Timmy, dear God. Help the doctors and the nurses to know just what to do for him. Keep him from being afraid. Help him to heal so he can come back from the hospital very soon. In Jesus' name. Amen."

In the course of this brief activity the child has been introduced to thanksgiving, petition, confession, and intercession. In due course, children will learn to form their own short prayers, with the adult asking only the leading questions, followed perhaps by, "Now how will you talk to God about this?"

Even if adults in the family and in the congregation they attend still use the language forms of centuries ago (hath, hast, thee, thou, thine, vouchsafe, deign) my bias is against imposing these on children. I would first teach children the Lord's Prayer in its contemporary ecumenical version (see page 156), so that prayer does not seem to them to be some odd event that requires knowledge of a special language used nowhere else. And I would frame all other prayers in the same accessible terms. By overhearing, children will gradually learn some of the older forms as needed, and then may decide whether or not to use them in their own prayers.

My rationale stems from my own upbringing. I grew up in a heavily Germanic town in Illinois. My grandparents' generation could speak German, and preferred to do so. My parents' generation could understand German when they heard it, but they did not speak it. My generation could neither speak it nor understand it. With respect to the old language forms of English, the church today is pretty much in the middle generation but well on its way to the third generation. No matter how beautiful "King James English" may be to the ear, in most congregations it has a first generation character that intimidates even adults into silence when the leader of worship says: "I invite you now to offer your own prayers aloud." (Oh dear! What if I use "thee" when I should use "thy"? I'll just keep quiet so as not to embarrass myself.) Knowing fully that some will disagree with me, I strongly encourage that children be taught to address God in the same vocabulary used to address one another.

Very few prayers written specifically for use by children exist, and some that do need to be examined closely. The popular "Now I lay me down to sleep" prayer raises several typical issues. First, its form is not actually that of a prayer. It is a statement about what the child is doing, not a petition of what the child asks God to do. Were it petition, it would read: "O Lord, as I lie down to sleep, watch over me...." Second, the content is restricted to the child; the only pronouns are "I," "me," and "my." Are not children sufficiently egocentric without reinforcing this tendency through memorized prayers? Finally, while prayer certainly should partake of reality, is it the best of ideas to give a child this bedtime thought, "If I should die before I wake"? The prayers we teach children should not saddle them for years to come with incorrect forms, selfish theology, or intimidating fears. If a readily memorized rhyming quatrain is desired, something like this would be more suitable:

Dear God, protect us through the night
and wake us with the morning light;
Then give us all another day
to walk within your loving way.

Throughout the process of teaching children to pray, care should be taken to expand their horizons of human concern and their capacity to trust in a gracious God, to enable them to see prayer as conversation with a God who nurtures a profound divine-human friendship.

VIII. Lectionary

SUNDAY READINGS
On Sundays, three readings are given, drawn from the Revised Common Lectionary, widely used as the basis for preaching the Scriptures systematically. This is a system spread across three years as follows:

Year A begins on the First Sunday in Advent of calendar years that are divisible by 3 (Advent of 2004, 2007, 2010 ...)

Year B then begins in Advent of 2005, 2008, 2011 ...

Year C begins in Advent of 2006, 2009, 2012 ...

WEEKDAY READINGS
Monday through Saturday readings are based on a system that extends across two years:

Year One begins in Advent of odd-numbered years (2005, 2007, 2009 ...)

Year Two begins in Advent of even-numbered years (2004, 2006, 2008 ...)

On certain occasions in the weekday readings, selections from the Apocrypha are used. Note particularly the difference between Ecclesiastes (abbreviated Eccles.) in the Old Testament and Ecclesiasticus (abbreviated Ecclus.) in the Apocrypha. In all cases where portions of the Apocrypha are assigned, alternative Old Testament readings are given for those who do not have, or prefer not to use, the Apocrypha. It is worth noting that in the New Testament period many Jews used the texts of the Apocrypha for sacred reading and study and the church therefore did likewise. Ultimately, however, the texts of the Apocrypha were not adopted as Scripture by Judaism; at the time of the Reformation many Protestants (though not all) deleted them, causing the Old Testament of the church to conform to the canon of the synagogue. Even so, much that is in the Apocrypha is edifying to Christians, and portions of these texts are again being used for devotional purposes. Hence their inclusion here.

+ + +

ADVENT

During Advent we rejoice in the promise of Christ's coming, both in the flesh at Bethlehem and in glory at the end of time.

Advent begins on the fourth Sunday prior to December 25. It varies from twenty-two to twenty-eight days in length. Readings are provided for four full weeks; in Week 4 you will delete certain readings when Advent is not twenty-eight days long.

WEEK 1 OF ADVENT

Sunday A	Isa. 2:1-5	Rom. 13:11-14	Matt. 24:36-44
B	Isa. 64:1-9	1 Cor. 3:1-9	Mark 13:24-37
C	Jer. 33:14-16	1 Thess. 3:9-13	Luke 21:25-36

Weekdays, Year One

Monday	Isa. 1:10-20	1 Thess. 1:1-10	Luke 20:1-8
Tuesday	Isa. 1:21-31	1 Thess. 2:1-12	Luke 20:9-18
Wednesday	Isa. 2:1-11	1 Thess. 2:13-20	Luke 20:19-26
Thursday	Isa. 2:12-22	1 Thess. 3:1-13	Luke 20:27-40
Friday	Isa. 3:8-15	1 Thess. 4:1-12	Luke 20:41–21:4
Saturday	Isa. 4:2-6	1 Thess. 4:13-18	Luke 21:5-19

Weekdays, Year Two

Monday	Amos 2:6-16	2 Pet. 1:1-11	Matt. 21:1-11
Tuesday	Amos 3:1-11	2 Pet. 1:12-21	Matt. 21:12-22
Wednesday	Amos 3:12–4:5	2 Pet. 3:1-10	Matt. 21:23-32
Thursday	Amos 4:6-13	2 Pet. 3:11-18	Matt. 21:33-46
Friday	Amos 5:1-17	Jude 1-16	Matt. 22:1-14
Saturday	Amos 5:18-27	Jude 17-25	Matt. 22:15-22

WEEK 2 OF ADVENT

Sunday A	Isa. 11:1-10	Rom. 15:4-13	Matt. 3:1-12
B	Isa. 40:1-11	2 Pet. 3:8-15a	Mark 1:1-8
C	Mal. 3:1-4	Phil. 3:1-11	Luke 3:1-6

Weekdays, Year One

Monday	Isa. 5:8-12, 18-23	1 Thess. 5:1-11	Luke 21:20-28
Tuesday	Isa. 5:13-17, 24-25	1 Thess. 5:12-28	Luke 21:29-38
Wednesday	Isa. 6:1-13	2 Thess. 1:1-12	John 7:53–8:11
Thursday	Isa. 7:1-9	2 Thess. 2:1-12	Luke 22:1-13
Friday	Isa. 7:10-25	2 Thess. 2:13–3:5	Luke 22:14-30
Saturday	Isa. 8:1-15	2 Thess. 3:6-18	Luke 22:31-38

Weekdays, Year Two

Monday	Amos 7:1-9	Rev. 1:1-8	Matt. 22:23-33
Tuesday	Amos 7:10-17	Rev. 1:9-16	Matt. 22:34-46
Wednesday	Amos 8:1-14	Rev. 1:17–2:7	Matt. 23:1-12
Thursday	Amos 9:1-10	Rev. 2:8-17	Matt. 23:13-26
Friday	Haggai 1:1-15	Rev. 2:18-29	Matt. 23:27-39
Saturday	Haggai 2:1-9	Rev. 3:1-6	Matt. 24:1-14

WEEK 3 OF ADVENT

Sunday A	Isa. 35:1-10	James 5:7-10	Matt. 11:2-11
B	Isa. 61:1-4, 8-11	1 Thess. 5:16-24	John 1:6-8, 19-28
C	Zeph. 3:14-20	Phil. 4:4-7	Luke 3:7-18

Weekdays, Year One

Monday	Isa. 8:16–9:1	2 Pet. 1:1-11	Luke 22:39-53
Tuesday	Isa. 9:1-7	2 Pet. 1:12-21	Luke 22:54-69
Wednesday	Isa. 9:8-17	2 Pet. 2:1-10a	Mark 1:1-8
Thursday	Isa. 9:18–10:4	2 Pet. 2:10b-16	Matt. 3:1-12
Friday	Isa. 10:5-19	2 Pet. 2:17-22	Matt. 11:2-15
Saturday	Isa. 10:20-27	Jude 17-25	Luke 3:1-9

Weekdays, Year Two

Monday	Zech. 1:7-17	Rev. 3:7-13	Matt. 24:15-31
Tuesday	Zech. 2:1-13	Rev. 3:14-22	Matt. 24:32-44
Wednesday	Zech. 3:1-10	Rev. 4:1-8	Matt. 24:45-51
Thursday	Zech. 4:1-14	Rev. 4:9–5:5	Matt. 25:1-13
Friday	Zech. 7:8–8:8	Rev. 5:6-14	Matt. 25:14-30
Saturday	Zech. 8:9-17	Rev. 6:1-17	Matt. 25:31-46

WEEK 4 OF ADVENT

Sunday A	Isa. 7:10-16	Rom. 1:1-7	Matt. 1:18-25
B	2 Sam. 7:1-11, 16	Rom. 16:25-27	Luke 1:26-38
C	Micah 5:2-5a	Heb. 10:5-10	Luke 1:39-45

Hereafter use as many weekday readings as needed to extend to December 23. Then follow the dated occasions listed under "Christmas." (See page 182.)

Weekdays, Year One

Monday	Isa. 11:1-9	Rev. 20:1-10	John 5:30-47
Tuesday	Isa. 11:10-16	Rev. 20:11–21:8	Luke 1:5-25
Wednesday	Isa. 28:9-22	Rev. 21:9-21	Luke 1:26-38
Thursday	Isa. 29:13-24	Rev. 21:22–22:5	Luke 1:39-56

| Friday | Isa. 33:17-22 | Rev. 22:6-11, 28-20 | Luke 1:57-66 |

Weekdays, Year Two

Monday	Zeph. 3:14-20	Titus 1:1-16	Luke 1:1-25
Tuesday	1 Sam. 2:1b-10	Titus 2:1-10	Luke 1:26-38
Wednesday	2 Sam. 7:1-17	Titus 2:11–3:8a	Luke 1:39-56
Thursday	2 Sam. 7:18-29	Gal. 3:1-14	Luke 1:57-66
Friday	Baruch 4:21-29, or Jer. 31:10-14	Gal. 3:15-22	Luke 1:67-80

CHRISTMAS

At Christmas the church remembers that God has come among us, accepting our nature in order to give us divine grace. The events of Jesus' nativity, epiphany, and baptism reveal to us who he is.

Christmas Day proclaims the humble appearing of God in our midst, announced to Jewish shepherds, a people often looked upon with suspicion and disdain because they were nomadic. The Epiphany (a Greek term meaning "manifestation" or "revelation") recalls the visit of learned Gentiles, whose gifts identify Jesus as ruler of all (gold), deity (frankincense), and one who suffers and dies (myrrh). At his baptism, Jesus is proclaimed from heaven to be God's own Son, the one in whom God delights.

Listed first here are readings for three Sundays related to Christmas Day. Then follow weekday readings, listed by calendar dates, beginning with Christmas Eve Day.

FIRST SUNDAY AFTER CHRISTMAS DAY (between December 26 and 30, inclusive)

Sunday A	Isa 63:7-9	Heb. 2:10-18	Matt. 2:13-23
B	Isa. 61:10–62:3	Gal. 4:4-7	Luke 2:22-40
C	1 Sam. 2:18-20,26	Col. 3:12-17	Luke 2:41-52

When December 25 is a Sunday, the next Sunday (January 1) is The Epiphany.

THE EPIPHANY (Sunday between December 31 and 6, inclusive)

| Sunday A, B, C | Isa. 60:1-6 | Eph. 3:1-12 | Matt. 2:1-12 |

BAPTISM OF THE LORD (Sunday between January 7 and 13, inclusive)

| Sunday A | Isa. 42:1-9 | Acts 10:34-43 | Matt. 3:13-17 |
| B | Gen. 1:1-5 | Acts 19:1-7 | Mark 1:4-11 |

C	Isa. 43:1-7	Acts 8:14-17	Luke 3:15-17, 21-22

Year One

December 24	Isa. 35:1-10	Rev. 22:12-17, 21	Luke 1:67-80
December 25	Zech. 2:10-13	1 John 4:7-16	Luke 2:1-7
December 26	Wis. 4:7-15, or 2 Chron. 24:17-22	Gal. 3:24–4:7	John 3:31-36
December 27	Prov. 8:22-30	1 John 5:1-12	John 13:20-35
December 28	Isa. 49:13-23	Col. 1:9-20	Matt. 18:1-14
December 29	Isa. 12:1-6	Rev. 1:1-8	John 7:37-52
December 30	Isa. 25:1-9	Rev. 1:19-20	John 7:53–8:11
December 31	Isa. 26:1-9	2 Cor. 5:16–6:2	John 8:12-19
January 1	Gen. 17:1-12a, 15-16	Col. 2:6-12	Luke 2:21 (or 21-40)

Note that January 1 marks the circumcision and naming of Jesus on the eighth day of his life among us.

January 2	Gen. 12:1-7	Heb. 11:1-12	John 6:35-42, 48-51
January 3	Gen. 28:10-22	Heb. 11:13-22	John 10:7-17
January 4	Exod. 3:1-5	Heb. 11:23-31	John 14:6-14
January 5	Joshua 1:1-9	Heb. 11:32–12:2	John 15:1-16
January 6	Isa. 52:7-10	Rev. 21:22-27	Matt. 12:14-21

Readings for dated occasions that follow are used only through Saturday of this week. On Sunday use the readings above for the Baptism of the Lord.

January 7	Isa. 52:3-6	Rev. 2:1-7	John 2:1-11
January 8	Isa. 59:15b-21	Rev. 2:8-17	John 4:46-54
January 9	Isa. 63:1-5	Rev. 2:18-29	John 5:1-15
January 10	Isa. 65:1-9	Rev. 3:1-6	John 6:1-14
January 11	Isa. 65:13-16	Rev. 3:7-13	John 6:15-27
January 12	Isa. 66:1-2, 22-23	Rev. 3:14-22	John 9:1-12, 35-38

Year Two

December 24	Isa. 60:1-6	Gal. 3:15-22	Matt. 1:18-25
December 25	Micah 4:1-5	1 John 4:7-16	Luke 2:8-20
December 26	Wis. 4:7-15, or 2 Chron. 24:17-22	Gal. 3:24–4:7	John 3:31-36
December 27	Prov. 8:22-30	1 John 5:1-12	John 13:20-35

December 28	Isa. 49:13-23	Col. 1:9-20	Matt. 18:1-14
December 29	2 Sam. 23:13-17	Rev. 1:1-8	John 7:37-52
December 30	1 Kings 17:17-24	3 John 1-15	John 4:46-54
December 31	1 Kings 3:5-14	James 4:13-17, 5:7-11	John 5:1-15
January 1	Isa. 62:1-5	Rev. 19:1-16	Matt. 1:18-25

Note that January 1 marks the circumcision and naming of Jesus on the eighth day of his life among us.

January 2	1 Kings 19:1-8	Eph. 4:1-16	John 6:1-14
January 3	1 Kings 19:9-18	Eph. 4:17-32	John 6:15-27
January 4	Joshua 3:14–4:7	Eph. 5:1-20	John 9:1-12, 35-38
January 5	Jonah 2:2-9	Eph. 6:10-20	John 11:17-27, 38-44
January 6	Isa. 49:1-7	Rev. 21:22-27	Matt. 12:14-21

Readings for dated occasions that follow are used only through Saturday of this week. On Sunday use the readings above for the Baptism of the Lord. (See pages 182-83.)

January 7	Deut. 8:1-3	Col. 1:1-14	John 6:30-33, 48-51
January 8	Exod. 17:1-7	Col. 1:15-23	John 7:37-52
January 9	Isa. 45:14-19	Col. 1:24–2:7	John 8:12-19
January 10	Jer. 23:1-8	Col. 2:8-23	John 10:7-17
January 11	Isa. 55:3-9	Col. 3:1-17	John 14:6-14
January 12	Gen. 49:1-2, 8-12	Col. 3:18–4:6	John 15:1-16

Immediately after the Sunday of the Baptism of the Lord, proceed with the weeks listed below until the Sunday of the Transfiguration (which is the Sunday prior to Ash Wednesday).

Transfiguration Sunday occurs as follows:

2005	February 6	2010	February 14
2006	February 26	2011	March 6
2007	February 18	2012	February 19
2008	February 3	2013	Feburary 10
2009	February 22	2014	March 2

Weekdays following the Sunday of the Baptism of the Lord (see above):

Weekdays, Year One

Monday	Isa. 40:12-24	Eph. 1:1-14	Mark 1:1-13
Tuesday	Isa. 40:25-31	Eph. 1:15-23	Mark 1:14-28

Wednesday	Isa. 41:1-16	Eph. 2:1-10	Mark 1:29-45
Thursday	Isa. 41:17-29	Eph. 2:11-22	Mark 2:1-12
Friday	Isa. 42:1-17	Eph. 3:1-13	Mark 2:13-22
Saturday	Isa. 43:11-25	Eph. 3:14-21	Mark 2:23–3:6

Weekdays, Year Two

Monday	Gen. 2:4-25	Heb. 1:1-14	John 1:1-18
Tuesday	Gen. 3:1-24	Heb. 2:1-10	John 1:19-28
Wednesday	Gen. 4:1-16	Heb. 2:11-18	John 1:29-42
Thursday	Gen. 4:17-26	Heb. 3:1-11	John 1:43-51
Friday	Gen. 6:1-8	Heb. 3:12-19	John 2:1-12
Saturday	Gen. 6:9-22	Heb. 4:1-13	John 2:13-22

SUNDAY BETWEEN JANUARY 14 and 20, inclusive

Sunday A	Isa. 49:1-7	1 Cor. 1:1-9	John 1:29-42
B	1 Sam. 3:1-20	1 Cor. 6:12-20	John 1:43-51
C	Isa. 62:1-5	1 Cor. 12:1-11	John 2:1-11

Weekdays, Year One

Monday	Isa. 44:6-8, 21-23	Eph. 4:1-16	Mark 3:7-19a
Tuesday	Isa. 44:9-20	Eph. 4:17-32	Mark 3:19b-35
Wednesday	Isa. 44:24–45:7	Eph. 5:1-14	Mark 4:1-20
Thursday	Isa. 45:5-17	Eph. 5:15-33	Mark 4:21-34
Friday	Isa. 45:18-25	Eph. 6:1-9	Mark 4:35-41
Saturday	Isa. 46:1-13	Eph. 6:10-24	Mark 5:1-20

Weekdays, Year Two

Monday	Gen. 8:6-22	Heb. 4:14–5:6	John 2:23–3:15
Tuesday	Gen. 9:1-17	Heb. 5:7-14	John 3:16-21
Wednesday	Gen. 9:18-29	Heb. 6:1-12	John 3:22-36
Thursday	Gen. 11:1-9	Heb. 6:13-20	John 4:1-15
Friday	Gen. 11:27–12:8	Heb. 7:1-17	John 4:16-26
Saturday	Gen. 12:9–13:1	Heb. 7:18-28	John 4:27-42

SUNDAY BETWEEN JANUARY 21 and 27, inclusive

Sunday A	Isa. 9:1-4	1 Cor. 1:10-18	Matt. 4:12-23
B	Jonah 3:1-5, 10	1 Cor. 7:29-31	Mark 1:14-20
C	Neh. 8:1-3, 5-6, 8-10	1 Cor. 12:12-31	Luke 4:14-21

Weekdays, Year One

| Monday | Isa. 48:1-11 | Gal. 1:1-17 | Mark 5:21-43 |
| Tuesday | Isa. 48:12-22 | Gal. 1:18–2:10 | Mark 6:1-13 |

Wednesday	Isa. 49:1-12	Gal. 2:11-21	Mark 6:13-29
Thursday	Isa. 49:13-26	Gal. 3:1-14	Mark 6:30-46
Friday	Isa. 50:1-11	Gal. 3:15-22	Mark 6:47-56
Saturday	Isa. 51:1-8	Gal. 3:23-29	Mark 7:1-23

Weekdays, Year Two

Monday	Gen. 14:1-24	Heb. 8:1-13	John 4:43-54 8-24
Tuesday	Gen. 15:1-21	Heb. 9:1-14	John 5:1-18
Wednesday	Gen. 16:1-14	Heb. 9:15-28	John 5:19-29
Thursday	Gen. 16:15–17:14	Heb. 10:1-10	John 5:30-47
Friday	Gen. 17:15-27	Heb. 10:11-25	John 6:1-15
Saturday	Gen. 18:1-16	Heb. 10:26-39	John 6:16-27

SUNDAY BETWEEN JANUARY 28 and FEBRUARY 3, inclusive, unless this is the Sunday immediately before Lent.
Then see readings for Transfiguration Sunday, page 189.

Sunday A	Micah 6:1-8	1 Cor. 1:18-31	Matt. 5:1-12
B	Deut. 18:15-20	1 Cor. 8:1-13	Mark 1:21-28
C	Jer. 1:4-10	1 Cor. 13:1-13	Luke 4:21-30

Weekdays, Year One

Monday	Isa. 51:17-23	Gal. 4:1-11	Mark 7:24-37
Tuesday	Isa. 52:1-12	Gal. 4:12-20	Mark 8:1-10
Wednesday	Isa. 54:1-10	Gal. 4:21-31	Mark 8:11-17
Thursday	Isa. 55:1-13	Gal. 5:1-15	Mark 8:27–9:1
Friday	Isa. 56:1-8	Gal. 5:16-24	Mark 9:2-13
Saturday	Isa. 57:3-13	Gal. 5:25–6:10	Mark 9:14-29

Weekdays, Year Two

Monday	Gen. 19:1-23	Heb. 11:1-12	John 6:27-40
Tuesday	Gen. 21:1-21	Heb. 11:13-22	John 6:41-51
Wednesday	Gen. 22:1-18	Heb. 11:23-31	John 6:52-59
Thursday	Gen. 23:1-20	Heb. 11:32–12:2	John 6:60-71
Friday	Gen. 24:1-27	Heb. 12:3-11	John 7:1-13
Saturday	Gen. 24:28-38	Heb. 12:12-29	John 7:14-36, 49-51

SUNDAY BETWEEN FEBRUARY 4 and 10, inclusive, unless this is the Sunday immediately before Lent.
Then see readings for Transfiguration Sunday, page 189.

| Sunday A | Isa. 58:1-12 | 1 Cor. 2:1-16 | Matt. 5:13-20 |

B	Isa. 40:21-31	1 Cor. 9:16-23	Mark 1:29-39
C	Isa. 6:1-13	1 Cor. 15:1-11	Luke 5:1-11

Weekdays, Year One

Monday	Isa. 58:1-12	Gal. 6:11-18	Mark 9:30-41
Tuesday	Isa. 59:1-15a	2 Tim. 1:1-14	Mark 9:42-50
Wednesday	Isa. 59:15b-21	2 Tim. 1:15–2:13	Mark 10:1-16
Thursday	Isa. 60:1-17	2 Tim. 2:14-26	Mark 10:17-31
Friday	Isa. 61:1-9	2 Tim. 3:1-17	Mark 10:32-45
Saturday	Isa. 61:10–62:5	2 Tim. 4:1-8	Mark 10:46-52

Weekdays, Year Two

Monday	Gen. 25:19-34	Heb. 13:1-16	John 7:37-52
Tuesday	Gen. 26:1-6	Heb. 13:17-25	John 7:53–8:11
Wednesday	Gen. 27:1-29	Rom. 12:1-8	John 8:12-20
Thursday	Gen. 27:30-45	Rom. 12:9-21	John 8:21-32
Friday	Gen. 27:46–28:4, 10-22	Rom. 13:1-14	John 8:33-47
Saturday	Gen. 29:1-20	Rom. 14:1-23	John 8:47-59

SUNDAY BETWEEN FEBRUARY 11 and 17, inclusive, unless this is the Sunday immediately before Lent.
Then see readings for Transfiguration Sunday, page 189.

Sunday A	Deut. 30:15-20	1 Cor. 3:1-9	Matt. 5:21-37
B	2 Kings 5:1-14	1 Cor. 9:24-27	Mark 1:40-45
C	Jer. 17:5-10	1 Cor. 15:12-20	Luke 6:17-26

Weekdays, Year One

Monday	Isa. 63:1-6	1 Tim. 1:1-17	Mark 11:1-11
Tuesday	Isa. 63:7-14	1 Tim. 1:18–2:15	Mark 11:12-26
Wednesday	Isa. 63:15–64:9	1 Tim. 3:1-16	Mark 11:27–12:12
Thursday	Isa. 65:1-12	1 Tim. 4:1-16	Mark 12:13-27
Friday	Isa. 65:17-25	1 Tim. 5:1-25	Mark 12:28-34
Saturday	Isa. 66:1-6	1 Tim. 6:1-21	Mark 12:35-44

Weekdays, Year Two

Monday	Gen. 30:1-24	1 John 1:1-10	John 9:1-17
Tuesday	Gen. 31:1-24	1 John 2:1-11	John 9:18-41
Wednesday	Gen. 31:25-50	1 John 2:12-17	John 10:1-18
Thursday	Gen. 32:3-21	1 John 2:18-29	John 10:19-30
Friday	Gen. 32:22–33:17	1 John 3:1-10	John 10:31-42
Saturday	Gen. 35:1-20	1 John 3:11-18	John 11:1-16

SUNDAY BETWEEN FEBRUARY 18 and 24, inclusive, unless this is the
Sunday immediately before Lent.
Then see readings for Transfiguration Sunday, page 189.

Sunday A	Lev. 19:1-2, 9-18	1 Cor. 3:10-11, 16-23	Matt. 5:38-48
B	Isa. 43:18-25	2 Cor. 1:18-22	Mark 2:1-12
C	Gen. 45:3-11, 15	1 Cor. 15:35-38, 42-50	Luke 6:27-38

Weekdays, Year One

Monday	Ruth 1:1-14	2 Cor. 1:1-11	Matt. 5:1-12
Tuesday	Ruth 1:15-22	2 Cor. 1:12-22	Matt. 5:13-20
Wednesday	Ruth 2:1-13	2 Cor. 1:23–2:17	Matt. 5:21-26
Thursday	Ruth 2:14-23	2 Cor. 3:1-18	Matt. 5:27-37
Friday	Ruth 3:1-18	2 Cor. 4:1-12	Matt. 5:38-48
Saturday	Ruth 4:1-22	2 Cor. 4:13–5:10	Matt. 6:1-16

Weekdays, Year Two

Monday	Prov. 3:11-20	1 John 3:18–4:6	John 11:17-29
Tuesday	Prov. 4:1-27	1 John 4:7-21	John 11:30-44
Wednesday	Prov. 6:1-19	1 John 5:1-12	John 11:45-54
Thursday	Prov. 7:1-27	1 John 5:13-21	John 11:55–12:8
Friday	Prov. 8:1-21	Philemon 1-25	John 12:9-19
Saturday	Prov. 8:22-36	2 Tim. 1:1-14	John 12:20-26

SUNDAY BETWEEN FEBRUARY 25 and 29, inclusive, unless this is the
Sunday immediately before Lent.
Then see readings for Transfiguration Sunday, page 189.

Sunday A	Isa. 49:8-16a	1 Cor. 4:1-5	Matt. 6:24-34
B	Hosea 2:14-20	2 Cor. 3:1-6	Mark 2:13-22
C	Isa. 55:10-13	1 Cor. 15:51-58	Luke 6:39-49

Weekdays, Year One

Monday	Deut. 4:9-14	2 Cor. 10:1-18	Matt. 6:7-15
Tuesday	Deut. 4:15-24	2 Cor. 11:1-21a	Matt. 6:16-23
Wednesday	Deut. 4:25-31	2 Cor. 11:21b-33	Matt. 6:24-34
Thursday	Deut. 4:32-40	2 Cor. 12:1-10	Matt. 7:1-12
Friday	Deut. 5:1-22	2 Cor. 12:11-21	Matt. 7:13-21
Saturday	Deut. 5:22-33	2 Cor. 13:1-14	Matt. 7:22-29

Weekdays, Year Two

Monday	Prov. 10:1-12	2 Tim. 1:15–2:13	John 12:27-36a
Tuesday	Prov. 15:16-33	2 Tim. 2:14-26	John 12:36b-50

Wednesday	Prov. 17:1-20	2 Tim. 3:1-17	John 13:1-20
Thursday	Prov. 21:30–22:6	2 Tim. 4:1-8	John 13:21-30
Friday	Prov. 23:19-21, 29–24:2	2 Tim. 4:9-22	John 13:31-38
Saturday	Prov. 25:15-28	Phil. 1:1-11	John 18:1-14

LENT

Lent is a time of forty weekdays of devotion. Six Sundays are not included in the count. For the Lord's Day is always a feast day, never an occasion for fasting or the kind of introspection that characterizes this season.

In the ancient church Lent was the time when those who were to be baptized at Easter made their final preparation for membership. Hence Lent is a time for intensified prayer, fasting, and study by all who have been previously baptized. Its themes are transformation and renewal made possible by divine covenant love as attested in our sacred history.

The season begins with Ash Wednesday, a day that reminds us of our weakness and mortality, a day on which we make open confession of our sin and seek God's mercy.

In recent decades a number of denominations have begun to celebrate the transfiguration of Jesus on the Sunday before Ash Wednesday, for the transfiguration is a transitional event between Christmas and Easter, which helps us identify who it is who was born in a manger and is on his journey toward the cross.

TRANSFIGURATION SUNDAY (the last Sunday before Lent)

Sunday A	Exod. 24:12-18	2 Pet. 1:16-21	Matt. 17:1-9
B	2 Kings 2:1-12	2 Cor. 4:3-6	Mark 9:2-9
C	Exod. 34:29-35	2 Cor. 3:12–4:2	Luke 9:28-43

Weekdays, Year One

Monday	Deut. 6:1-15	Heb. 1:1-14	John 1:1-18
Tuesday	Deut. 6:16-25	Heb. 2:1-10	John 1:19-28
Ash Wednesday	Jonah 3:1–4:11	Heb. 12:1-14	Luke 18:9-14
Thursday	Deut. 7:6-11	Titus 1:1-16	John 1:29-34
Friday	Deut. 7:12-16	Titus 2:1-15	John 1:35-42
Saturday	Deut. 7:17-26	Titus 3:1-15	John 1:43-51

Weekdays, Year Two

Monday	Prov. 27:1-6, 10-12	Phil. 2:1-13	John 18:15-18, 25-27

Tuesday	Prov. 30:1-4, 24-33	Phil. 3:1-11	John 18:28-38
Ash Wednesday	Amos 5:6-15	Heb. 12:1-14	Luke 18:9-14
Thursday	Hab. 3:1-18	Phil. 3:12-21	John 17:1-18
Friday	Ezek. 18:1-4, 25-32	Phil. 4:1-9	John 17:9-19
Saturday	Ezek. 39:21-29	Phil. 4:10-20	John 17:20-26

WEEK OF FIRST SUNDAY IN LENT

Sunday A	Gen. 2:15-17, 3:1-7	Rom. 5:12-19	Matt. 4:1-11
B	Gen. 9:8-17	1 Pet. 3:18-22	Mark 1:9-15
C	Deut. 26:1-11	Rom. 10:8b-13	Luke 4:1-13

Weekdays, Year One

Monday	Deut. 8:11-20	Heb. 2:11-18	John 2:1-12
Tuesday	Deut. 9:4-12	Heb. 3:1-11	John 2:13-22
Wednesday	Deut. 9:13-21	Heb. 3:12-19	John 2:23–3:15
Thursday	Deut. 9:23–10:5	Heb. 4:1-10	John 3:16-21
Friday	Deut. 10:12-22	Heb. 4:11-16	John 3:22-36
Saturday	Deut. 11:18-28	Heb. 5:1-10	John 4:1-26

Weekdays, Year Two

Monday	Gen. 37:1-11	1 Cor. 1:1-19	Mark 1:1-13
Tuesday	Gen. 37:12-24	1 Cor. 1:20-31	Mark 1:14-28
Wednesday	Gen. 37:25-36	1 Cor. 2:1-13	Mark 1:29-45
Thursday	Gen. 39:1-23	1 Cor. 2:14–3:15	Mark 2:1-12
Friday	Gen. 40:1-23	1 Cor. 3:16-23	Mark 2:13-22
Saturday	Gen. 41:1-13	1 Cor. 4:1-7	Mark 2:23–3:6

WEEK OF SECOND SUNDAY IN LENT

Sunday A	Gen. 12:1-4a	Rom. 4:1-5, 13-17	John 3:1-17
B	Gen. 17:1-7, 15-16	Rom. 4:13-25	Mark 8:31-38
C	Gen. 15:1-12, 17-18	Phil. 3:17–4:1	Luke 13:31-35

Weekdays, Year One

Monday	Jer. 1:11-19	Rom. 1:1-15	John 4:27-42
Tuesday	Jer. 2:1-13	Rom. 1:16-25	John 4:43-54
Wednesday	Jer. 3:6-18	Rom. 1:28–2:11	John 5:1-18
Thursday	Jer. 4:9-10, 19-28	Rom. 2:12-24	John 5:19-29
Friday	Jer. 5:1-9	Rom. 2:25–3:18	John 5:30-47
Saturday	Jer. 5:20-31	Rom. 3:19-31	John 7:1-13

Weekdays, Year Two

Monday	Gen. 41:46-57	1 Cor. 4:8-21	Mark 3:7-19a
Tuesday	Gen. 42:1-17	1 Cor. 5:1-8	Mark 3:19b-35
Wednesday	Gen. 42:18-28	1 Cor. 5:9–6:8	Mark 4:1-20
Thursday	Gen. 42:29-38	1 Cor. 6:12-20	Mark 4:21-34
Friday	Gen. 43:1-15	1 Cor. 7:1-9	Mark 4:35-41
Saturday	Gen. 43:16-34	1 Cor. 7:10-24	Mark 5:1-20

WEEK OF THIRD SUNDAY IN LENT

Sunday A	Exod. 17:1-7	Rom. 5:1-11	John 4:5-42
B	Exod. 20:1-17	1 Cor. 1:18-25	John 2:13-22
C	Isa. 55:1-9	1 Cor. 10:1-13	Luke 13:1-9

Weekdays, Year One

Monday	Jer. 7:1-15	Rom. 4:1-12	John 7:14-36
Tuesday	Jer. 7:21-34	Rom. 4:13-25	John 7:37-52
Wednesday	Jer. 8:4-7, 18–9:6	Rom. 5:1-11	John 8:12-20
Thursday	Jer. 10:11-24	Rom. 5:12-21	John 8:21-32
Friday	Jer. 11:1-8, 14-20	Rom. 6:1-11	John 8:33-47
Saturday	Jer. 13:1-11	Rom. 6:12-23	John 8:47-59

Weekdays, Year Two

Monday	Gen. 44:18-34	1 Cor. 7:25-31	Mark 5:21-43
Tuesday	Gen. 45:1-15	1 Cor. 7:32-40	Mark 6:1-13
Wednesday	Gen. 45:16-28	1 Cor. 8:1-13	Mark 6:13-29
Thursday	Gen. 46:1-7, 28-34	1 Cor. 9:1-15	Mark 6:30-46
Friday	Gen. 47:1-26	1 Cor. 9:16-27	Mark 6:47-56
Saturday	Gen. 47:27–48:7	1 Cor. 10:1-13	Mark 7:1-23

WEEK OF FOURTH SUNDAY IN LENT

Sunday A	1 Sam. 16:1-13	Eph. 5:8-14	John 9:1-41
B	Num. 21:4-9	Eph. 2:1-10	John 3:14-21
C	Joshua 5:9-12	2 Cor. 5:16-21	Luke 5:1-3, 11b-32

Weekdays, Year One

Monday	Jer. 16:1-21	Rom. 7:1-12	John 6:1-15
Tuesday	Jer. 17:19-27	Rom. 7:13-25	John 6:16-27
Wednesday	Jer. 18:1-11	Rom. 8:1-11	John 6:27-40
Thursday	Jer. 22:13-23	Rom. 8:12-27	John 6:41-51
Friday	Jer. 23:1-8	Rom. 8:28-39	John 6:52-59
Saturday	Jer. 23:9-15	Rom. 9:1-18	John 6:60-71

Weekdays, Year Two

Monday	Gen. 49:1-28	1 Cor. 10:14–11:1	Mark 7:24-37
Tuesday	Gen. 49:29–50:14	1 Cor. 11:2-34	Mark 8:1-10
Wednesday	Gen. 50:15-26	1 Cor. 12:1-11	Mark 8:11-26
Thursday	Exod. 1:6-22	1 Cor. 12:12-26	Mark 8:27–9:1
Friday	Exod. 2:1-22	1 Cor. 12:27–13:3	Mark 9:2-13
Saturday	Exod. 2:23–3:15	1 Cor. 13:1-13	Mark 9:14-29

WEEK OF FIFTH SUNDAY IN LENT

Sunday A	Ezek. 37:1-14	Rom. 8:6-11	John 11:1-45
B	Jer. 31:31-34	Heb. 5:5-10	John 12:20-33
C	Isa. 43:16-21	Phil. 3:4b-14	John 12:1-8

Weekdays, Year One

Monday	Jer. 24:1-10	Rom. 9:19-33	John 9:1-17
Tuesday	Jer. 25:8-17	Rom. 10:1-13	John 9:18-41
Wednesday	Jer. 25:30-38	Rom. 10:14-21	John 10:1-18
Thursday	Jer. 26:1-24	Rom. 11:1-12	John 10:19-42
Friday	Jer. 29:1-14	Rom. 11:13-24	John 11:1-27 or 12:1-10
Saturday	Jer. 31:27-34	Rom. 11:25-36	John 11:28-44 or 12:37-50

Weekdays, Year Two

Monday	Exod. 4:10-26	1 Cor. 14:1-19	Mark 9:30-41
Tuesday	Exod. 5:1–6:1	1 Cor. 14:20-33a	Mark 9:42-50
Wednesday	Exod. 7:8-24	2 Cor. 2:14–3:6	Mark 10:1-16
Thursday	Exod. 7:25–8:19	2 Cor. 3:7-18	Mark 10:17-31
Friday	Exod. 9:13-35	2 Cor. 4:1-12	Mark 10:32-45
Saturday	Exod. 10:21–11:8	2 Cor. 4:13-18	Mark 10:46-52

WEEK OF SIXTH SUNDAY IN LENT (Palm-Passion Sunday), also called Holy Week

Sunday A	Isa. 50:4-9a	Phil. 2:5-11	Matt. 26:14–27:66
B	Isa. 50:4-9a	Phil. 2:5-11	Mark 14:1–15:47
C	Isa. 50:4-9a	Phil. 2:5-11	Luke 22:14–23:49

Weekdays, Year One

Monday	Jer. 12:1-16	Phil. 3:1-14	John 12:9-19
Tuesday	Jer. 15:10-21	Phil. 3:15-21	John 12:20-26
Wednesday	Jer. 17:5-17	Phil. 4:1-13	John 12:27-26
Maundy			
Thursday	Jer. 20:7-18	1 Cor. 10:14-17	John 17:1-26
Good Friday	Wis. 1:16–2:1, 12:22 or Gen. 22:1-14	1 Pet. 1:10-20	John 13:36-38, 19:38-42
Holy Saturday	Job 19:21-27a	Heb. 4:1-16	Rom. 8:1-11

Weekdays, Year Two

Monday	Lam. 1:1-2, 6-12	2 Cor. 1:1-7	Mark 11:12-25
Tuesday	Lam. 1:17-22	2 Cor. 1:8-22	Mark 11:27-33
Wednesday	Lam. 2:1-9	2 Cor. 1:23–2:11	Mark 12:1-11
Maundy			
Thursday	Lam. 2:10-18	1 Cor. 10:14-17	Mark 14:12-25
Good Friday	Lam. 3:1-9, 19-33	1 Pet. 1:10-20	John 13:36-38, 19:38-42
Holy Saturday	Lam. 3:37-58	Heb. 4:1-16	Rom. 8:1-11

EASTER

The Great Fifty Days from Easter Day through the Day of Pentecost celebrate the resurrection of the Lord and the hope we have of being raised with him. Furthermore, we think during this period about the nature of the church as a resurrection community.

EASTER WEEK

Easter Day A	Acts 10:34-43	Col. 3:1-4	John 20:1-18, or Matt. 28:1-10
B	Acts 10:34-43	1 Cor. 15:1-11	John 20:1-18, or Mark 16:1-8
C	Acts 10:34-43	1 Cor. 15:19-26	John 20:1-18, or Luke 24:1-12

Weekdays, Year One

Monday	Jonah 2:1-10	Acts 2:14, 22-32	John 14:1-14
Tuesday	Isa. 30:18-26	Acts 2:26-47	John 14:15-31
Wednesday	Micah 7:7-15	Acts 3:1-10	John 15:1-11
Thursday	Ezek. 37:1-14	Acts 3:11-26	John 15:12-27
Friday	Dan. 12:1-4, 13	Acts 4:1-12	John 16:1-15
Saturday	Isa. 25:1-9	Acts 4:13-31	John 16:16-33

Weekdays, Year Two

Monday	Exod. 12:14-27	1 Cor. 15:1-11	Mark 16:1-8
Tuesday	Exod. 12:28-39	1 Cor. 15:12-28	Mark 16:9-20
Wednesday	Exod. 12:40-51	1 Cor. 15:29-41	Matt. 28:1-16
Thursday	Exod. 13:3-10	1 Cor. 15:41-50	Matt. 28:16-20
Friday	Exod. 13:1-2, 11-16	1 Cor. 15:51-58	Luke 24:1-12
Saturday	Exod. 13:17–14:4	2 Cor. 4:16–5:10	Mark 12:18-27

SECOND WEEK OF EASTER

Sunday A	Acts 2:14a, 22-32	1 Pet. 1:3-9	John 20:19-31
B	Acts 4:32-35	1 John 1:1–2:2	John 20:19-31
C	Acts 5:27-32	Rev. 1:4-8	John 20:19-31

Weekdays, Year One

Monday	Dan. 1:1-21	1 John 1:1-10	John 17:1-11
Tuesday	Dan. 2:1-16	1 John 2:1-11	John 17:12-19
Wednesday	Dan. 2:17-30	1 John 2:12-17	John 17:20-26
Thursday	Dan. 2:31-49	1 John 2:18-29	Luke 3:1-14
Friday	Dan 3:1-18	1 John 3:1-10	Luke 3:15-22
Saturday	Dan. 3:19-30	1 John 3:11-18	Luke 4:1-13

Weekdays, Year Two

Monday	Exod. 14:21-31	1 Pet. 1:1-12	John 14:1-17
Tuesday	Exod. 15:1-21	1 Pet. 1:13-25	John 14:18-31
Wednesday	Exod. 15:22–16:10	1 Pet. 2:1-10	John 15:1-11
Thursday	Exod. 16:10-22	1 Pet. 2:11–3:12	John 15:12-27
Friday	Exod. 16:23-36	1 Pet. 3:13–4:6	John 16:1-15
Saturday	Exod. 17:1-16	1 Pet. 4:7-19	John 16:16-33

THIRD WEEK OF EASTER

Sunday A	Acts 2:14a, 36-41	1 Pet. 1:17-23	Luke 24:13-35
B	Acts 3:12-19	1 John 3:1-7	Luke 24:36b-48
C	Acts 9:1-20	Rev. 5:11-14	John 21:1-19

Weekdays, Year One

Monday	Dan. 4:19-27	1 John 3:19–4:6	Luke 4:14-30
Tuesday	Dan. 4:28-37	1 John 4:7-21	Luke 4:31-37
Wednesday	Dan. 5:1-12	1 John 5:1-12	Luke 4:38-44
Thursday	Dan. 5:13-30	1 John 5:13-21	Luke 5:1-11

| Friday | Dan. 6:1-15 | 2 John 1-13 | Luke 5:12-26 |
| Saturday | Dan. 6:16-28 | 3 John 1-15 | Luke 5:27-39 |

Weekdays, Year Two

Monday	Exod. 18:13-27	1 Pet. 5:1-14	Matt. 3:1-6
Tuesday	Exod. 19:1-16	Col. 1:1-14	Matt. 3:7-12
Wednesday	Exod. 19:16-25	Col. 1:15-23	Matt. 3:13-17
Thursday	Exod. 20:1-21	Col. 1:24–2:7	Matt. 4:1-11
Friday	Exod. 24:1-18	Col. 2:8-23	Matt. 4:12-17
Saturday	Exod. 25:1-22	Col. 3:1-17	Matt. 4:18-25

FOURTH WEEK OF EASTER

Sunday A	Acts 2:42-27	1 Pet. 2:19-25	John 10:1-10
B	Acts 4:5-12	1 John 3:16-24	John 10:11-18
C	Acts 9:36-43	Rev. 7:9-17	John 10:22-30

Weeksdays, Year One

Monday	Wis. 1:16–2:11, 21-24 or Jer. 30:1-9	Col. 1:1-14	Luke 6:1-11
Tuesday	Wis. 3:1-9 or Jer. 30:10-17	Col. 1:15-23	Luke 6:12-26
Wednesday	Wis. 4:16–5:8 or Jer. 30:18-22	Col. 1:24–2:7	Luke 6:27-38
Thursday	Wis. 5:9-23 or Jer. 31:1-14	Col. 2:8-23	Luke 6:39-49
Friday	Wis. 6:12-23 or Jer. 31:15-22	Col. 3:1-11	Luke 7:1-17
Saturday	Wis. 7:1-14 or Jer. 31:23-25	Col. 3:12-17	Luke 7:18-35

Weekdays, Year Two

Monday	Exod. 32:1-20	Col. 3:18–4:6	Matt. 5:1-10
Tuesday	Exod. 32:21-34	1 Thess. 1:1-10	Matt. 5:11-16
Wednesday	Exod. 33:1-23	1 Thess. 2:1-12	Matt. 5:17-20
Thursday	Exod. 34:1-17	1 Thess. 2:13-20	Matt. 5:21-26
Friday	Exod. 34:18-35	1 Thess. 3:1-13	Matt. 5:27-37
Saturday	Exod. 40:18-38	1 Thess. 4:1-12	Matt. 5:38-48

FIFTH WEEK OF EASTER

Sunday A	Acts 7:55-60	1 Pet. 2:2-10	John 14:1-14
B	Acts 8:26-40	1 John 4:7-21	John 15:1-8
C	Acts 11:1-18	Rev. 21:1-6	John 13:31-35

Weekdays, Year One

Monday	Wis. 9:1, 7-18 or Jer. 32:1-15	Col. 3:18–4:18	Luke 7:36-50
Tuesday	Wis. 10:1-4 or Jer. 32:16-25	Rom. 12:1-21	Luke 8:1-15
Wednesday	Wis. 13:1-9 or Jer. 32:36-44	Rom. 13:1-14	Luke 8:16-25
Thursday	Wis. 14:27–15:3 or Jer. 33:1-13	Rom. 14:1-12	Luke 8:26-39
Friday	Wis. 16:15–17:1 or Jer. 33:14-26	Rom. 14:13-23	Luke 8:40-56
Saturday	Wis. 19:1-8, 18-22 or Deut. 31:30–32:14	Rom. 15:1-13	Luke 9:1-17

Weekdays, Year Two

Monday	Lev. 16:1-19	1 Thess. 4:13-18	Matt. 6:1-6, 16-18
Tuesday	Lev. 16:20-34	1 Thess. 5:1-11	Matt. 6:7-15
Wednesday	Lev. 19:1-18	1 Thess. 5:12-28	Matt. 6:19-24
Thursday	Lev. 19:26-37	2 Thess. 1:1-12	Matt. 6:25-34
Friday	Lev. 23:1-22	2 Thess. 2:1-17	Matt. 7:1-12
Saturday	Lev. 23:23-44	2 Thess. 3:1-18	Matt. 7:13-21

SIXTH WEEK OF EASTER

Sunday A	Acts 17:22-31	I Pet. 3:13-22	John 14:15-21
B	Acts 10:44-48	1 John 5:1-16	John 15:9-17
C	Acts 16:9-15	Rev. 21:10, 22–22:5	John 14:23-29

Weekdays, Year One

Monday	Deut. 8:1-10	James 1:1-15	Luke 8:18-27
Tuesday	Deut. 8:11-20	James 1:16-27	Luke 11:1-13
Wednesday	Baruch 3:24-37 or Deut. 19:1-7	James 5:13-18	Luke 12:22-31
Ascension Day	Ezek. 1:1-14, 24-28b	Heb. 2:5-18	Matt. 28:16-20
Friday	Ezek. 1:28–3:3	Heb. 4:14–5:6	Luke 9:28-36
Saturday	Ezek. 3:4-17	Heb. 5:7-14	Luke 9:37-50

Weekdays, Year Two

Monday	Lev. 25:35-55	Col. 1:9-14	Matt. 13:1-16
Tuesday	Lev. 26:1-20	1 Tim. 2:1-6	Matt. 13:18-23
Wednesday	Lev. 26:27-42	Eph. 1:1-10	Matt. 22:41-46
Ascension Day	Dan. 7:9-14	Heb. 2:5-18	Matt. 28:16-20
Friday	1 Sam. 2:1-10	Eph. 2:1-10	Matt. 7:22-27

Saturday	Num. 11:16-17, 24-29	Eph. 2:11-22	Matt. 7:28–8:4

SEVENTH WEEK OF EASTER

Sunday A	Acts 1:6-14	1 Pet. 4:12-14, 5:6-11	John 17:1-11
B	Acts 1:15-17, 21-26	1 John 5:9-13	John 17:6-19
C	Acts 16:16-34	Rev. 22:12-14, 16-17, 20-21	John 17:20-26

Weekdays, Year One

Monday	Ezek. 4:1-17	Heb. 6:1-12	Luke 9:51-62
Tuesday	Ezek. 7:10-15, 23b-27	Heb. 6:13-20	Luke 10:1-17
Wednesday	Ezek. 11:14-25	Heb. 7:1-17	Luke 10:17-24
Thursday	Ezek. 18:1-4, 19-32	Heb. 7:18-28	Luke 10:25-37
Friday	Ezek. 34:17-31	Heb. 8:1-13	Luke 10:38-42
Saturday	Ezek. 43:1-12	Heb. 9:1-14	Luke 11:14-23

Weekdays, Year Two

Monday	Joshua 1:1-9	Eph. 3:1-13	Matt. 8:5-17
Tuesday	1 Sam. 16:1-13a	Eph. 3:14-21	Matt. 8:18-27
Wednesday	Isa. 4:2-6	Eph. 4:1-16	Matt. 8:28-34
Thursday	Zech. 4:1-14	Eph. 4:17-32	Matt. 9:1-8
Friday	Jer. 31:27-34	Eph. 5:1-20	Matt. 9:9-17
Saturday	Ezek. 36:22-27	Eph. 6:10-24	Matt. 9:18-26

PENTECOST SUNDAY (and days of the week following in certain years)

Sunday A	Acts 2:1-21	1 Cor. 12:3b-13	John 7:37-39
B	Acts 2:1-21	Rom. 8:22-27	John 15:26-27, 16:4b-15
C	Acts 2:1-21	Rom. 8:14-17	John 14:8-27

If Pentecost Sunday falls between May 10 and 16, inclusive, the following weekday readings are used. If Pentecost Sunday falls later (as it will in most years) use the weekday readings from the tables of dated weeks below.

Weekdays, Year One

Monday	Isa. 63:7-14	2 Tim. 1:1-14	Luke 11:24-36
Tuesday	Isa. 63:15–64:9	2 Tim. 1:15–2:13	Luke 11:37-52
Wednesday	Isa. 65:1-12	2 Tim. 2:14-26	Luke 11:53–12:12

Thursday	Isa. 65:17-25	2 Tim. 3:1-17	Luke 12:13-31
Friday	Isa. 66:1-6	2 Tim. 4:1-8	Luke 12:32-48
Saturday	Isa. 66:7-14	2 Tim. 4:9-22	Luke 12:49-59

Weekdays, Year Two

Monday	Ezek. 33:1-11	1 John 1:1-10	Matt. 9:27-34
Tuesday	Ezek. 33:21-33	1 John 2:1-11	Matt. 9:35–10:4
Wednesday	Ezek. 34:1-16	1 John 2:12-17	Matt. 10:5-15
Thursday	Ezek. 37:21b-28	1 John 2:18-29	Matt. 10:16-23
Friday	Ezek. 39:21-29	1 John 3:1-10	Matt. 10:24-33
Saturday	Ezek. 47:1-12	1 John 3:11-18	Matt. 10:34-42

TRINITY SUNDAY (Sunday after the Day of Pentecost)

Sunday A	Gen. 1:1–2:4a	2 Cor. 13:11-13	Matt. 28:16-20
B	Isa. 6:1-8	Rom. 8:12-17	John 3:1-17
C	Prov. 8:1-4, 22-31	Rom. 5:1-5	John 16:12-15

Find the date of Trinity Sunday in the tables below and use the weekday readings given there.

After Trinity Sunday continue to use the dated Sunday and weekday readings until the beginning of Advent.

SUNDAY BETWEEN MAY 17 and 23, inclusive, if after Pentecost Sunday

Weekdays, Year One

Monday	Ruth 1:1-18	1 Tim. 1:1-17	Luke 13:1-9
Tuesday	Ruth 1:19–2:13	1 Tim. 1:18–2:8	Luke 13:10-17
Wednesday	Ruth 2:14-23	1 Tim. 3:1-16	Luke 13:18-30
Thursday	Ruth 3:1-18	1 Tim. 4:1-16	Luke 13:31-35
Friday	Ruth 4:1-22	1 Tim. 5:17-22	Luke 14:1-11
Saturday	Deut. 1:1-8	1 Tim. 6:6-21	Luke 14:12-24

Weekdays, Year Two

Monday	Prov. 3:11-20	1 John 3:18–4:6	Matt. 11:1-6
Tuesday	Prov. 4:1-27	1 John 4:7-21	Matt. 11:7-15
Wednesday	Prov. 6:1-19	1 John 5:1-12	Matt. 11:16-24
Thursday	Prov. 7:1-27	1 John 5:13-21	Matt. 11:25-30
Friday	Prov. 8:1-21	2 John 1-13	Matt. 12:1-14
Saturday	Prov. 8:22-36	3 John 1-15	Matt. 12:15-21

SUNDAY BETWEEN MAY 24 and 28, inclusive, if after Pentecost Sunday

Sunday A	Isa. 49:8-16a	1 Cor. 4:1-5	Matt. 6:24-34
B	Hosea 2:14-20	2 Cor. 3:1-6	Mark 2:13-22
C	Isa. 55:10-13	1 Cor. 15:51-58	Luke 6:39-49

If this is Trinity Sunday, use Sunday readings for that occasion instead, as listed above. Use weekday readings below after Trinity Sunday.

Weekdays, Year One

Monday	Deut. 4:9-14	2 Cor. 1:1-11	Luke 14:25-35
Tuesday	Deut. 4:15-24	2 Cor. 1:12-22	Luke 15:1-10
Wednesday	Deut. 4:25-31	2 Cor. 1:23–2:17	Luke 15:1-2, 11-32
Thursday	Deut. 4:32-40	2 Cor. 3:1-18	Luke 16:1-9
Friday	Deut. 5:1-22	2 Cor. 4:1-12	Luke 16:10-18
Saturday	Deut. 5:22-33	2 Cor. 4:13–5:10	Luke 16:19-31

Weekdays, Year Two

Monday	Prov. 10:1-12	1 Tim. 1:1-17	Matt. 12:22-32
Tuesday	Prov. 15:16-33	1 Tim. 1:18–2:15	Matt. 12:33-42
Wednesday	Prov. 17:1-20	1 Tim. 3:1-16	Matt. 12:43-50
Thursday	Prov. 21:30–22:6	1 Tim. 4:1-16	Matt. 13:24-30
Friday	Prov. 23:19-21, 29–24:2	1 Tim. 5:17-25	Matt. 13:31-35
Saturday	Prov. 25:15-28	1 Tim. 6:6-21	Matt. 13:36-43

SUNDAY BETWEEN MAY 29 and JUNE 4, inclusive, if after Pentecost
Sunday

Sunday A	Gen. 6:9-22, 7:24, 8:14-19	Rom. 1:16-17, 3:22b-31	Matt. 7:21-29
B	1 Sam. 3:1-20	2 Cor. 4:5-12	Mark 2:23–3:6
C	1 Kings 18:20-39	Gal. 1:1-12	Luke 7:1-10

If this is Trinity Sunday, use Sunday readings for that occasion instead, as listed above. Use weekday readings below after Trinity Sunday.

Weekdays, Year One

Monday	Deut. 11:13-19	2 Cor 5:11–6:2	Luke 17:1-10
Tuesday	Deut. 12:1-12	2 Cor. 6:3-13, 7:1	Luke 17:11-19
Wednesday	Deut. 13:1-11	2 Cor. 7:2-16	Luke 17:20-37
Thursday	Deut. 16:18-20, 17:14-20	2 Cor. 8:1-16	Luke 18:1-8
Friday	Deut. 26:1-11	2 Cor. 8:16-24	Luke 18:9-14
Saturday	Deut. 29:2-15	2 Cor. 9:1-15	Luke 18:15-30

Weekdays, Year Two

Monday	Eccles. 2:1-15	Gal. 1:1-17	Matt. 13:44-52
Tuesday	Eccles. 2:16-26	Gal. 1:18–2:10	Matt. 13:53-58
Wednesday	Eccles. 3:1-15	Gal. 2:11-21	Matt. 14:1-12

Thursday	Eccles. 3:16–4:3	Gal. 3:1-14	Matt. 14:13-21
Friday	Eccles. 5:1-7	Gal. 3:15-22	Matt. 14:22-36
Saturday	Eccles. 5:8-20	Gal. 3:23–4:11	Matt. 15:1-20

SUNDAY BETWEEN JUNE 5 and 11, inclusive, if after Pentecost Sunday

Sunday A	Gen. 12:1-9	Rom. 4:13-25	Matt. 9:9-26
B	1 Sam. 8:4-20, 11:14-15	2 Cor. 4:13–5:1	Mark 3:20-35
C	1 Kings 17:8-24	Gal. 1:11-24	Luke 7:11-17

If this is Trinity Sunday, use Sunday readings for that occasion instead, as listed above. Use weekday readings below after Trinity Sunday.

Weekdays, Year One

Monday	Deut. 30:1-10	2 Cor. 10:1-18	Luke 18:31-43
Tuesday	Deut. 30:11-20	2 Cor. 11:1-21a	Luke 19:1-10
Wednesday	Deut. 31:30–32:14	2 Cor. 11:21b-33	Luke 19:11-27
Thursday	Ecclus. 44:19–45:5 or S. of Sol. 1:1-3, 9-11, 15-16a, 2:1-3a	2 Cor. 12:1-10	Luke 19:28-40
Friday	Ecclus. 45:6-16 or S. of Sol. 2:8-13, 4:1-4a, 5-7, 9-11	2 Cor. 12:11-21	Luke 19:41-48
Saturday	Ecclus. 46:1-10 or S. of Sol. 5:10-16, 7:1-7a, 8:6-7	2 Cor. 13:1-14	Luke 20:1-8

Weekdays, Year Two

Monday	Eccles. 7:1-14	Gal. 4:12-20	Matt. 15:21-28
Tuesday	Eccles. 8:14–9:10	Gal. 4:21-31	Matt. 15:29-39
Wednesday	Eccles. 9:11-18	Gal. 5:1-15	Matt. 16:1-12
Thursday	Eccles. 11:1-8	Gal. 5:16-24	Matt. 16:13-20
Friday	Eccles. 11:9–12:14	Gal. 5:25–6:10	Matt. 16:21-28
Saturday	Num. 3:1-13	Gal. 6:11-18	Matt. 17:1-13

SUNDAY BETWEEN JUNE 12 and 18, inclusive, if after Pentecost Sunday

Sunday A	Gen. 18:1-15	Rom. 5:1-8	Matt. 9:35-10:23
B	1 Sam. 15:34–16:13	2 Cor. 5:6-17	Mark 4:26-34
C	1 Kings 21:1-21a	Gal. 2:15-21	Luke 7:36–8:3

If this is Trinity Sunday, use Sunday readings for that occasion instead, as listed above, and weekday readings below for the week following.

Weekdays, Year One

Monday	1 Sam. 1:1-20	Acts 1:1-14	Luke 20:9-19
Tuesday	1 Sam. 1:21–2:11	Acts 1:15-26	Luke 20:19-26
Wednesday	1 Sam. 2:12-26	Acts 2:1-21	Luke 20:27-40
Thursday	1 Sam. 2:27-36	Acts 2:22-36	Luke 20:41–21:4
Friday	1 Sam. 3:1-21	Acts 2:37-47	Luke 21:5-19
Saturday	1 Sam. 4:1b-11	Acts 4:32–5:11	Luke 21:20-28

Weekdays, Year Two

Monday	Num. 9:15-23, 10:29-36	Rom. 1:1-15	Matt. 17:14-21
Tuesday	Num. 11:1-23	Rom. 1:16-25	Matt. 17:22-27
Wednesday	Num. 11:24-35	Rom. 1:28–2:11	Matt. 18:1-9
Thursday	Num. 12:1-16	Rom. 2:12-24	Matt. 18:10-20
Friday	Num. 13:1-3, 21-30	Rom. 2:25–3:8	Matt. 18:21-35
Saturday	Num. 13:31–14:25	Rom. 3:9-20	Matt. 19:1-12

SUNDAY BETWEEN JUNE 19 and 25, inclusive

Sunday A	Gen. 21:8-21	Rom. 6:1b-11	Matt. 10:24-39
B	1 Sam. 17:1b, 4-11, 19-23, 32-49	2 Cor. 6:1-13	Mark 4:35-41
C	1 Kings 19:1-15a	Gal. 3:23-29	Luke 8:26-39

If this is Trinity Sunday, use Sunday readings for that occasion instead, as listed above, and weekday readings below for the week following.

Weekdays, Year One

Monday	1 Sam. 5:1-12	Acts 5:12-26	Luke 21:29-36
Tuesday	1 Sam. 6:1-16	Acts 5:27-42	Luke 21:37–22:13
Wednesday	1 Sam. 7:2-17	Acts 6:1-15	Luke 22:14-23
Thursday	1 Sam. 8:1-22	Acts 6:15–7:16	Luke 22:24-30
Friday	1 Sam. 9:1-14	Acts 7:17-29	Luke 22:31-38
Saturday	1 Sam. 9:15–10:1	Acts 7:30-43	Luke 22:39-51

Weekdays, Year Two

Monday	Num. 16:1-19	Rom. 3:21-31	Matt. 19:13-22
Tuesday	Num. 16:20-35	Rom. 4:1-12	Matt. 19:23-30
Wednesday	Num. 16:36-50	Rom. 4:13-25	Matt. 20:1-16

Thursday	Num. 17:1-11	Rom. 5:1-11	Matt. 20:17-28
Friday	Num. 20:1-13	Rom. 5:12-21	Matt. 20:29-34
Saturday	Num. 20:14-29	Rom. 6:1-11	Matt. 21:1-11

SUNDAY BETWEEN JUNE 26 and JULY 2, inclusive

Sunday A	Gen. 22:1-14	Rom. 6:12-23	Matt. 10:40-42
B	2 Sam. 1:1, 17-27	2 Cor. 8:7-15	Mark 5:21-43
C	2 Kings 2:1-2, 6-14	Gal. 5:1, 13-25	Luke 9:51-62

Weekdays, Year One

Monday	1 Sam. 10:17-27	Acts 7:44–8:1a	Luke 22:52-62
Tuesday	1 Sam. 11:1-15	Acts 8:1b-13	Luke 22:63-71
Wednesday	1 Sam. 12:1-25	Acts 8:14-25	Luke 23:1-12
Thursday	1 Sam. 13:5-18	Acts 8:26-40	Luke 23:13-25
Friday	1 Sam. 13:19–14:15	Acts 9:1-9	Luke 23:26-31
Saturday	1 Sam. 14:16-30	Acts 9:10-19a	Luke 23:32-43

Weekdays, Year Two

Monday	Num. 22:1-21	Rom. 6:12-23	Matt. 21:12-22
Tuesday	Num. 22:21-40	Rom. 7:1-12	Matt. 21:23-32
Wednesday	Num. 22:41–23:12	Rom. 7:13-25	Matt. 21:33-46
Thursday	Num. 23:11-30	Rom. 8:1-11	Matt. 22:1-14
Friday	Num. 24:1-13	Rom. 8:12-17	Matt. 22:15-22
Saturday	Num. 24:12-25	Rom. 8:18-25	Matt. 22:23-40

SUNDAY BETWEEN JULY 3 and 9, inclusive

Sunday A	Gen. 24:34-38, 42-49, 58-67	Rom. 7:15-25a	Matt. 11:16-19, 25-30
B	2 Sam. 5:1-5, 9-10	2 Cor. 12:2-10	Mark 6:1-13
C	2 Kings 5:1-14	Gal. 6:1-16	Luke 10:1-11, 16-20

Weekdays, Year One

Monday	1 Sam. 15:1-3, 7-23	Acts 9:19b-31	Luke 23:44-56a
Tuesday	1 Sam. 15:24-35	Acts 9:32-43	Luke 23:56b–24:11
Wednesday	1 Sam. 16:1-13	Acts 10:1-16	Luke 24:12-35
Thursday	1 Sam. 16:14–17:11	Acts 10:17-33	Luke 24:36-53

Friday	1 Sam. 17:17-30	Acts 10:34-48	Mark 1:1-13
Saturday	1 Sam. 17:31-49	Acts 11:1-18	Mark 1:14-28

Weekdays, Year Two

Monday	Num. 32:1-6, 16-27	Rom. 8:26-30	Matt. 23:1-12
Tuesday	Num. 35:1-3, 9-15, 30-34	Rom. 8:31-39	Matt. 23:13-26
Wednesday	Deut. 1:1-18	Rom. 9:1-18	Matt. 23:27-39
Thursday	Deut. 3:18-28	Rom. 9:19-33	Matt. 24:1-14
Friday	Deut. 31:7-13, 31:24–32:4	Rom. 10:1-13	Matt. 24:15-31
Saturday	Deut. 34:1-12	Rom. 10:14-21	Matt. 24:32-51

SUNDAY BETWEEN JULY 10 and 16, inclusive

Sunday A	Gen. 25:19-34	Rom. 8:1-11	Matt. 13:1-9, 18-23
B	2 Sam. 6:1-5, 12b-19	Eph. 1:3-14	Mark 6:14-29
C	Amos 7:7-17	Col. 1:1-14	Luke 10:25-37

Weekdays, Year One

Monday	1 Sam. 18:5-30	Acts 11:19-30	Mark 1:29-45
Tuesday	1 Sam. 19:1-24	Acts 12:1-17	Mark 2:1-12
Wednesday	1 Sam. 20:1-23	Acts 12:18-25	Mark 2:13-22
Thursday	1 Sam. 20:24-42	Acts 13:1-12	Mark 2:23–3:6
Friday	1 Sam. 21:1-15	Acts 13:13-25	Mark 3:7-19a
Saturday	1 Sam. 22:1-23	Acts 13:26-43	Mark 3:19b-35

Weekdays, Year Two

Monday	Joshua 2:1-14	Rom. 11:1-12	Matt. 25:1-13
Tuesday	Joshua 2:15-24	Rom. 11:13-24	Matt. 25:14-30
Wednesday	Joshua 3:1-13	Rom. 11:25-36	Matt. 25:31-46
Thursday	Joshua 3:14–4:7	Rom. 12:1-8	Matt. 26:1-16
Friday	Joshua 4:19–5:1, 10-15	Rom. 12:9-21	Matt. 26:17-25
Saturday	Joshua 6:1-14	Rom. 13:1-7	Matt. 26:26-35

SUNDAY BETWEEN JULY 17 and 23, inclusive

Sunday A	Gen. 28:10-19a	Rom. 8:12-25	Matt. 13:24-30, 36-43
B	2 Sam. 7:1-14a	Eph. 2:11-22	Mark 6:30-34, 53-56
C	Amos 8:1-12	Col. 1:15-28	Luke 10:38-42

Weekdays, Year One

Monday	1 Sam. 24:1-22	Acts 13:44-52	Mark 4:1-20
Tuesday	1 Sam. 25:1-22	Acts 14:1-18	Mark 4:21-34
Wednesday	1 Sam. 25:23-44	Acts 14:19-28	Mark 4:35-41
Thursday	1 Sam. 28:3-20	Acts 15:1-11	Mark 5:1-20
Friday	1 Sam. 31:1-13	Acts 15:12-21	Mark 5:21-43
Saturday	2 Sam. 1:1-16	Acts 15:22-35	Mark 6:1-13

Weekdays, Year Two

Monday	Joshua 7:1-13	Rom. 13:8-14	Matt. 26:36-46
Tuesday	Joshua 8:1-22	Rom. 14:1-12	Matt. 26:47-56
Wednesday	Joshua 8:30-35	Rom. 14:13-23	Matt. 26:57-68
Thursday	Joshua 9:3-21	Rom. 15:1-13	Matt. 26:69-75
Friday	Joshua 9:22–10:15	Rom. 15:14-24	Matt. 27:1-10
Saturday	Joshua 23:1-16	Rom. 15:25-33	Matt. 27:11-23

SUNDAY BETWEEN JULY 24 and 30, inclusive

Sunday A	Gen. 29:15-28	Rom. 8:26-39	Matt. 13:31-33, 44-52
B	2 Sam. 11:1-15	Eph. 3:14-21	John 6:1-21
C	Hosea 1:2-10	Col. 2:6-19	Luke 11:1-13

Weekdays, Year One

Monday	2 Sam. 2:1-11	Acts 15:36–16:5	Mark 6:14-29
Tuesday	2 Sam. 3:6-21	Acts 16:6-15	Mark 6:30-46
Wednesday	2 Sam. 3:22-39	Acts 16:16-24	Mark 6:47-56
Thursday	2 Sam. 4:1-12	Acts 16:25-40	Mark 7:1-23
Friday	2 Sam. 5:1-12	Acts 17:1-15	Mark 7:24-37
Saturday	2 Sam. 5:22–6:11	Acts 17:16-34	Mark 8:1-10

Weekdays, Year Two

Monday	Joshua 24:16-33	Rom. 16:1-16	Matt. 27:24-31
Tuesday	Judges 2:1-5, 11-23	Rom. 16:17-27	Matt. 27:32-44
Wednesday	Judges 3:12-30	Acts 1:1-14	Matt. 27:45-54
Thursday	Judges 4:4-23	Acts 1:15-26	Matt. 27:55-66
Friday	Judges 5:1-18	Acts 2:1-21	Matt. 28:1-10
Saturday	Judges 5:19-31	Acts 2:22-36	Matt. 28:11-20

SUNDAY BETWEEN JULY 31 and AUGUST 6, inclusive

Sunday A	Gen. 32:22-31	Rom. 9:1-5	Matt.14:13-21
B	2 Sam. 11:26–12:13a	Eph. 4:1-16	John 6:24-35
C	Hosea 11:1-11	Col. 3:1-11	Luke 12:13-21

Weekdays, Year One

Monday	2 Sam. 7:1-17	Acts 18:1-11	Mark 8:11-21
Tuesday	2 Sam. 7:18-29	Acts 18:12-28	Mark 8:22-33
Wednesday	2 Sam. 9:1-13	Acts 19:1-10	Mark 8:34–9:1
Thursday	2 Sam. 11:1-27	Acts 19:11-20	Mark 9:2-13
Friday	2 Sam. 12:1-14	Acts 19:21-41	Mark 9:14-29
Saturday	2 Sam. 12:15-31	Acts 20:1-16	Mark 9:30-41

Weekdays, Year Two

Monday	Judges 6:25-40	Acts 2:37-47	John 1:1-18
Tuesday	Judges 7:1-18	Acts 3:1-11	John 1:19-28
Wednesday	Judges 7:19–8:12	Acts 3:12-26	John 1:29-42
Thursday	Judges 8:22-35	Acts 4:1-12	John 1:43-51
Friday	Judges 9:1-16, 19-21	Acts 4:13-31	John 2:1-12
Saturday	Judges 9:22-25, 50-57	Acts 4:32–5:11	John 2:13-25

SUNDAY BETWEEN AUGUST 7 and 13, inclusive

Sunday A	Gen. 37:1-4, 12-28	Rom. 10:5-15	Matt. 14:22-33
B	2 Sam. 18:5-9, 15, 31-33	Eph. 4:25–5:2	John 6:35, 41-51
C	Isa. 1:1, 10-20	Heb. 11:1-3, 8-16	Luke 12:32-40

Weekdays, Year One

Monday	2 Sam. 13:23-39	Acts 20:17-38	Mark 9:42-50
Tuesday	2 Sam. 14:1-20	Acts 21:1-14	Mark 10:1-16
Wednesday	2 Sam. 14:21-33	Acts 21:15-26	Mark 10:17-31
Thursday	2 Sam. 15:1-18	Acts 21:27-36	Mark 10:32-45
Friday	2 Sam. 15:19-38	Acts 21:37–22:16	Mark 10:46-52
Saturday	2 Sam. 16:1-23	Acts 22:17-29	Mark 11:1-11

Weekdays, Year Two

Monday	Judges 12:1-7	Acts 5:12-26	John 3:1-21
Tuesday	Judges 13:1-15	Acts 5:27-42	John 3:22-36
Wednesday	Judges 13:15-24	Acts 6:1-15	John 4:1-26
Thursday	Judges 14:1-19	Acts 6:15–7:16	John 4:27-42
Friday	Judges 14:20–15:20	Acts 7:17-29	John 4:43-54
Saturday	Judges 16:1-14	Acts 7:30-43	John 5:1-18

SUNDAY BETWEEN AUGUST 14 and 20, inclusive

Sunday A	Gen. 45:1-15	Rom. 11:1-2a, 29-32	Matt. 15:10-28
B	1 Kings 2:10-12, 3:3-14	Eph. 5:15-20	John 6:51-58
C	Isa. 5:1-7	Heb. 11:29–12:2	Luke 12:49-56

Weekdays, Year One

Monday	2 Sam. 17:24–18:8	Acts 22:30–23:11	Mark 11:12-26
Tuesday	2 Sam.18:9-18	Acts 23:12-24	Mark 11:27–12:12
Wednesday	2 Sam. 18:19-33	Acts 23:23-35	Mark 12:13-27
Thursday	2 Sam. 19:1-23	Acts 24:1-23	Mark 12:28-34
Friday	2 Sam. 19:24-43	Acts 24:24–25:12	Mark 12:35-44
Saturday	2 Sam. 23:1-7, 13-17	Acts 28:17-31	Mark 13:1-13

Weekdays, Year Two

Monday	Judges 17:1-13	Acts 7:44–8:1a	John 5:19-29
Tuesday	Judges 18:1-15	Acts 8:1-13	John 5:30-47
Wednesday	Judges 18:16-31	Acts 8:14-25	John 6:1-15
Thursday	Job 1:1-22	Acts 8:26-40	John 6:16-27
Friday	Job 2:1-13	Acts 9:1-9	John 6:28-40
Saturday	Job 3:1-26	Acts 9:10-19a	John 6:41-51

SUNDAY BETWEEN AUGUST 21 and 27, inclusive

Sunday A	Exod. 1:8–2:10	Rom. 12:1-8	Matt. 16:13-20
B	1 Kings 8:1, 6, 10-11, 22-30, 41-43	Eph. 6:10-20	John 6:56-69
C	Jer. 1:4-10	Heb. 12:18-29	Luke 13:10-17

Weekdays, Year One

Monday	1 Kings 1:5-31	Acts 26:1-23	Mark 13:14-27
Tuesday	1 Kings 1:38–2:4	Acts 26:24–27:8	Mark 13:28-37
Wednesday	1 Kings 3:1-15	Acts 27:9-26	Mark 14:1-11
Thursday	1 Kings 3:16-28	Acts 27:27-44	Mark 14:12-26
Friday	1 Kings 5:1–6:1, 7	Acts 28:1-16	Mark 14:27-42
Saturday	1 Kings 7:51–8:21	Acts 28:17-31	Mark 14:43-52

Weekdays, Year Two

Monday	Job 4:1, 5:1-11, 17-21, 26-27	Acts 9:19b-31	John 6:52-59
Tuesday	Job 6:1-4, 8-15, 21	Acts 9:32-43	John 6:60-71
Wednesday	Job 6:1, 7:1-21	Acts 10:1-16	John 7:1-13
Thursday	Job 8:1-10, 20-22	Acts 10:17-33	John 7:14-36
Friday	Job 9:1-15, 32-35	Acts 10:34-48	John 7:37-52
Saturday	Job 9:1, 10:1-9, 16-22	Acts 11:1-18	John 8:12-20

SUNDAY BETWEEN AUGUST 28 and SEPTEMBER 3, inclusive

Sunday A	Exod. 3:1-15	Rom. 12:9-21	Matt. 16:21-28
B	S. of Sol. 2:8-13	James 1:17-27	Mark 7:1-8, 14-15, 21-23
C	Jer. 2:4-13	Heb. 13:1-8, 15-16	Luke 14:1, 7-14

Weekdays, Year One

Monday	1 Kings 8:22-64	James 2:1-13	Mark 14:53-65
Tuesday	1 Kings 8:65–9:9	James 2:14-26	Mark 14:66-72
Wednesday	1 Kings 9:24–10:13	James 3:1-12	Mark 15:1-11
Thursday	1 Kings 11:1-13	James 3:13–4:12	Mark 15:12-21
Friday	1 Kings 11:26-43	James 4:13–5:6	Mark 15:22-32
Saturday	1 Kings 12:1-20	James 5:7-20	Mark 15:33-39

Weekdays, Year Two

Monday	Job 12:1-6, 13-25	Acts 11:19-30	John 8:21-32
Tuesday	Job 12:1, 13:3-17, 21-27	Acts 12:1-17	John 8:33-47
Wednesday	Job 12:1, 14:1-22	Acts 12:18-25	John 8:48-59
Thursday	Job 16:16-22, 17:1, 13-16	Acts 13:1-12	John 9:1-17
Friday	Job 19:1-7, 14-27	Acts 13:13-25	John 9:18-41
Saturday	Job 22:1-4, 21–23:7	Acts 13:26-43	John 10:1-18

SUNDAY BETWEEN SEPTEMBER 4 and 10, inclusive

Sunday A	Exod. 12:1-14	Rom. 13:8-14	Matt. 18:15-20
B	Prov. 22:1-2, 8-9, 22-23	James 2:1-17	Mark 7:24-37
C	Jer. 18:1-11	Philemon 1-21	Luke 14:25-33

Weekdays, Year One

Monday	1 Kings 13:1-10	Phil. 1:1-11	Mark 15:40-47
Tuesday	1 Kings 16:23-34	Phil. 1:12-30	Mark 16:1-20
Wednesday	1 Kings 17:1-24	Phil. 2:1-11	Matt. 2:1-12
Thursday	1 Kings 18:1-19	Phil. 2:12-30	Matt. 2:13-23
Friday	1 Kings 18:20-40	Phil. 3:1-16	Matt. 3:1-12
Saturday	1 Kings 18:41–19:8	Phil. 3:17–4:23	Matt. 3:13-17

Weekdays, Year Two

Monday	Job 32:1-10, 19–33:1, 19-28	Acts 13:44-52	John 10:19-30
Tuesday	Job 29:1-20	Acts 14:1-18	John 10:31-42
Wednesday	Job 29:1, 30:1-2, 16-31	Acts 14:19-28	John 11:1-16
Thursday	Job 29:1, 31:1-23	Acts 15:1-11	John 11:17-29
Friday	Job 29:1, 31:24-40	Acts 15:12-21	John 11:30-44
Saturday	Job 38:1-17	Acts 15:22-35	John 11:45-54

SUNDAY BETWEEN SEPTEMBER 11 and 17, inclusive

Sunday A	Exod. 14:19-31	Rom. 14:1-12	Matt. 18:21-35
B	Prov. 1:20-33	James 3:1-12	Mark 8:27-38
C	Jer. 4:11-12, 22-28	1 Tim. 1:12-17	Luke 15:1-10

Weekdays, Year One

Monday	1 Kings 21:1-16	1 Cor. 1:1-19	Matt. 4:1-11
Tuesday	1 Kings 21:17-29	1 Cor. 1:20-31	Matt. 4:12-17
Wednesday	1 Kings 22:1-28	1 Cor. 2:1-13	Matt. 4:18-25
Thursday	1 Kings 22:29-45	1 Cor. 2:14–3:15	Matt. 5:1-10
Friday	2 Kings 1:2-17	1 Cor. 3:16-23	Matt. 5:11-16
Saturday	2 Kings 2:1-18	1 Cor. 4:1-7	Matt. 5:17-20

Weekdays, Year Two

Monday	Job 40:1-24	Acts 15:36–16:5	John 11:55–12:8
Tuesday	Job 40:1, 41:1-11	Acts 16:6-15	John 12:9-19
Wednesday	Job 42:1-17	Acts 16:16-24	John 12:20-26
Thursday	Job 28:1-28	Acts 16:25-40	John 12:27-36a
Friday	Esther 1:1-4, 10-19	Acts 17:1-15	John 12:36b-43
Saturday	Esther 2:5-8, 15-23	Acts 17:16-34	John 12:44-50

SUNDAY BETWEEN SEPTEMBER 18 and 24, inclusive

Sunday A	Exod. 16:2-15	Phil. 1:21-30	Matt. 20:1-16
B	Prov. 31:10-31	James 3:13–4:3, 7-8a	Mark 9:30-37
C	Jer. 8:18–9:1	1 Tim. 2:1-7	Luke 16:1-13

Weekdays, Year One

Monday	2 Kings 5:1-19a	1 Cor. 4:8-21	Matt. 5:21-26
Tuesday	2 Kings 5:19b-27	1 Cor. 5:1-8	Matt. 5:27-37
Wednesday	2 Kings 6:1-23	1 Cor. 5:9–6:8	Matt. 5:38-48
Thursday	2 Kings 9:1-16	1 Cor. 6:12-20	Matt. 6:1-6, 16-18
Friday	2 Kings 9:17-37	1 Cor. 7:1-9	Matt. 6:7-15
Saturday	2 Kings 11:1-20a	1 Cor. 7:10-24	Matt. 6:19-24

Weekdays, Year Two

Monday	Esther 4:4-17	Acts 18:1-11	Luke 3:1-14
Tuesday	Esther 5:1-14	Acts 18:12-28	Luke 3:15-22
Wednesday	Esther 6:1-14	Acts 19:1-10	Luke 4:1-13
Thursday	Esther 7:1-10	Acts 19:11-20	Luke 4:14-30
Friday	Esther 8:1-8, 15-17	Acts 19:21-41	Luke 4:31-37
Saturday	Esther 9:1–10:3	Acts 20:1-16	Luke 4:38-44

SUNDAY BETWEEN SEPTEMBER 25 and OCTOBER 1, inclusive

Sunday A	Exod. 17:1-7	Phil. 2:1-13	Matt. 21:23-32
B	Esther 7:1-6, 9-10, 9:20-22	James 5:13-20	Mark 9:38-50
C	Jer. 32:1-3a, 6-15	1 Tim. 6:6-19	Luke 16:19-31

Weekdays, Year One

Monday	2 Kings 17:24-41	1 Cor. 7:25-31	Matt. 6:25-34
Tuesday	2 Chron. 29:1-3, 30:1-27	1 Cor. 7:32-40	Matt. 7:1-12
Wednesday	2 Kings 18:9-25	1 Cor. 8:1-13	Matt. 7:13-21
Thursday	2 Kings 18:28-37	1 Cor. 9:1-15	Matt. 7:22-29
Friday	2 Kings 19:1-20	1 Cor. 9:16-27	Matt. 8:1-17
Saturday	2 Kings 19:21-36	1 Cor. 10:1-13	Matt. 8:18-27

Weekdays, Year Two

Monday	Hosea 1:1-11	Acts 20:17-38	Luke 5:1-11
Tuesday	Hosea 2:1-15	Acts 21:1-14	Luke 5:12-26
Wednesday	Hosea 2:16–3:5	Acts 21:15-26	Luke 5:27-39
Thursday	Hosea 4:1-10	Acts 21:27-36	Luke 6:1-11

Friday	Hosea 4:11-19	Acts 21:37–22:16	Luke 6:12-26
Saturday	Hosea 5:1-15	Acts 22:17-29	Luke 6:27-38

SUNDAY BETWEEN OCTOBER 2 and 8, inclusive

Sunday A	Exod. 20:1-4, 7-9, 12:20	Phil. 3:4b-14	Matt. 21:33-46
B	Job 1:1, 2:1-10	Heb. 1:1-4, 2:5-12	Mark 10:2-16
C	Lam. 1:1-6	2 Tim. 1:1-14	Luke 17:5-10

Weekdays, Year One

Monday	2 Kings 21:1-18	1 Cor. 10:14–11:1	Matt. 8:28-34
Tuesday	2 Kings 22:1-13	1 Cor. 11:2, 17-22	Matt. 9:1-8
Wednesday	2 Kings 22:14–23:3	1 Cor. 11:23-34	Matt. 9:9-17
Thursday	2 Kings 23:4-25	1 Cor. 12:1-11	Matt. 9:18-26
Friday	2 Kings 23:36–24:17	1 Cor. 12:12-26	Matt. 9:27-34
Saturday	Jer. 35:1-19	1 Cor. 12:27–13:3	Matt. 9:35–10:4

Weekdays, Year Two

Monday	Hosea 6:1–7:7	Acts 22:30–23:11	Luke 6:39-49
Tuesday	Hosea 7:8-16	Acts 23:12-24	Luke 7:1-17
Wednesday	Hosea 8:1-14	Acts 23:23-35	Luke 7:18-35
Thursday	Hosea 9:1-9	Acts 24:1-23	Luke 7:36-50
Friday	Hosea 9:10-17	Acts 24:24–25:12	Luke 8:1-15
Saturday	Hosea 10:1-15	Acts 25:13-27	Luke 8:16-25

SUNDAY BETWEEN OCTOBER 9 and 15, inclusive

Sunday A	Exod. 32:1-14	Phil. 4:1-9	Matt. 22:1-14
B	Job 23:1-9, 16-17	Heb. 4:12-16	Mark 10:17-31
C	Jer. 29:1, 4-7	2 Tim. 2:8-15	Luke 17:11-19

Weekdays, Year One

Monday	Jer. 36:1-26	1 Cor. 13:1-13	Matt. 10:5-15
Tuesday	Jer. 36:27–37:2	1 Cor. 14:1-12	Matt. 10:16-23
Wednesday	Jer. 37:3-21	1 Cor. 14:13-25	Matt. 10:24-33
Thursday	Jer. 38:1-13	1 Cor. 14:26-40	Matt. 10:34-42
Friday	Jer. 38:14-28	1 Cor. 15:1-11	Matt. 11:1-6
Saturday	Jer. 52:1-34	1 Cor. 15:12-29	Matt. 11:7-15

Weekdays, Year Two

Monday	Hosea 11:12–12:1	Acts 26:1-23	Luke 8:26-39
Tuesday	Hosea 12:2-14	Acts 26:24–27:8	Luke 8:40-56
Wednesday	Hosea 13:1-3	Acts 27:9-26	Luke 9:1-17
Thursday	Hosea 13:4-8	Acts 27:27-44	Luke 9:18-27
Friday	Hosea 13:9-16	Acts 28:1-16	Luke 9:28-36
Saturday	Hosea 14:1-9	Acts 28:17-31	Luke 9:37-50

SUNDAY BETWEEN OCTOBER 16 and 22, inclusive

Sunday A	Exod. 33:12-23	1 Thess. 1:1-10	Matt. 22:15-22
B	Job 38:1-7, 34-41	Heb. 5:1-10	Mark 10:35-45
C	Jer. 31:27-34	2 Tim. 3:14–4:5	Luke 18:1-8

Weekdays, Year One

Monday	Jer. 44:1-14	1 Cor. 15:30-41	Matt. 11:16-24
Tuesday	Lam. 1:1-12	1 Cor. 15:41-50	Matt. 11:25-30
Wednesday	Lam. 2:8-15	1 Cor. 15:51-58	Matt. 12:1-14
Thursday	Ezra 1:1-11	1 Cor. 16:1-9	Matt. 12:15-21
Friday	Ezra 3:1-13	1 Cor. 16:10-24	Matt. 12:22-32
Saturday	Ezra 4:7, 11-24	Philemon 1-25	Matt. 12:33-42

Weekdays, Year Two

Monday	Micah 1:1-16 or Ecclus. 4:1-10	Rev. 7:1-8	Luke 9:51-62
Tuesday	Micah 2:1-1 or Ecclus. 4:20–5:7	Rev. 7:9-17	Luke 10:1-16
Wednesday	Micah 3:1–4:10 or Ecclus. 7:4-14	Rev. 8:1-13	Luke 10:17-24
Thursday	Micah 4:11–5:15 or Ecclus. 10:1-18	Rev. 9:1-12	Luke 10:25-37
Friday	Micah 6:1-16 or Ecclus. 11:2-10	Rev. 9:13-21	Luke 10:38-42
Saturday	Micah 7:1-2 or Ecclus. 15:9-20	Rev. 10:1-11	Luke 11:1-13

SUNDAY BETWEEN OCTOBER 23 and 29, inclusive

Sunday A	Deut. 34:1-12	1 Thess. 2:1-8	Matt. 22:34-46
B	Job 42:1-6, 10-17	Heb. 7:23-28	Mark 10:46-52
C	Joel 2:23-32	2 Tim. 4:6-8, 16-18	Luke 18:9-14

Weekdays, Year One

Monday	Zech. 1:7-17	Rev. 1:1-20	Matt. 12:43-50

Tuesday	Ezra 5:1-17	Rev. 4:1-11	Matt. 13:1-9
Wednesday	Ezra 6:1-22	Rev. 5:1-10	Matt. 13:10-17
Thursday	Neh. 1:1-11	Rev. 5:11–6:11	Matt. 13:18-23
Friday	Neh. 2:1-20	Rev. 6:12–7:4	Matt. 13:24-30
Saturday	Neh. 4:1-23	Rev. 7:4-17	Matt. 13:31-35

Weekdays, Year Two

Monday	Jonah 1:1-17 or Ecclus. 19:4-17	Rev. 11:1-14	Luke 11:14-26
Tuesday	Jonah 2:1-10 or Ecclus. 24:1-12	Rev. 11:14-19	Luke 11:27-36
Wednesday	Jonah 3:1-10 or Ecclus. 28:14-26	Rev. 12:1-6	Luke 11:37-52
Thursday	Jonah 4:1-11 or Ecclus. 31:12-18	Rev. 12:7-17	Luke 11:53–12:12
Friday	Nahum 1:1–2:9 or Ecclus. 34:1-2, 22	Rev. 13:1-10	Luke 12:13-31
Saturday	Nahum 2:10–3:19 or Ecclus. 35:1-17	Rev. 13:11-18	Luke 12:32-48

SUNDAY BETWEEN OCTOBER 30 and NOVEMBER 5, inclusive

Sunday A	Joshua 3:7-17	1 Thess. 2:9-13	Matt. 23:1-12
B	Ruth 1:1-18	Heb. 9:11-14	Mark 12:28-34
C	Hab. 1:1-4, 2:1-4	2 Thess. 1:1-4, 11-12	Luke 19:1-10

OR

ALL SAINTS' SUNDAY (BETWEEN NOVEMBER 1 and 7, inclusive)
From earliest times, Christians honored those who died in faith.
Eventually November 1 was set aside as All Saints' Day for the joyful commemoration of the gracious work of Christ in all the faithful departed; from them we take instruction and inspiration. What they achieved in faith was not their own work but God's works shown forth through them. In many congregations All Saints' Day is observed on the first Sunday in November. In such cases the readings are:

Sunday A	Rev. 7:9-17	1 John 3:1-3	Matt. 5:1-12
B	Isa. 25:6-9	Rev. 21:1-6a	John 11:32-44
C	Dan. 7:1-3, 15-18	Eph. 1:11-23	Luke 6:20-31

In either case, the following weekday readings are used.

Weekdays, Year One

| Monday | Neh. 6:1-19 | Rev. 10:1-11 | Matt. 13:36-43 |
| Tuesday | Neh. 12:27-31a, 42b-47 | Rev. 11:1-19 | Matt. 13:44-52 |

Wednesday	Neh. 13:4-22	Rev. 12:1-12	Matt. 13:53-58
Thursday	Ezra 7:1-26	Rev. 14:1-13	Matt. 14:1-12
Friday	Ezra 7:27-28, 8:21-36	Rev. 15:1-8	Matt. 14:13-21
Saturday	Ezra 9:1-15	Rev. 17:1-14	Matt. 14:22-36

Weekdays, Year Two

Monday	Zeph. 1:1-13 or Ecclus. 38:24-34	Rev. 14:1-13	Luke 12:49-59
Tuesday	Zeph. 1:14-18 or Ecclus. 43:1-22	Rev. 14:14–15:8	Luke 13:1-9
Wednesday	Zeph. 2:1-15 or Ecclus. 43:23-33	Rev. 16:1-11	Luke 13:10-17
Thursday	Zeph. 3:1-7 or Ecclus. 44:1-15	Rev. 16:12-21	Luke 13:18-30
Friday	Zeph. 3:8-13 or Ecclus. 50:1, 11-24	Rev. 17:1-18	Luke 13:31-35
Saturday	Zeph. 3:14-20 or Ecclus. 51:1-12	Rev. 18:1-14	Luke 14:1-11

SUNDAY BETWEEN NOVEMBER 6 and 12, inclusive
If All Saints' Sunday is observed on November 6 or 7, see Sunday readings above.

Sunday A	Joshua 24:1-3a, 14-25	1 Thess. 4:13-18	Matt. 25:1-13
B	Ruth 3:1-5, 4:13-17	Heb. 9:24-28	Mark 12:38-44
C	Haggai 1:15b–2:9	2 Thess. 2:1-5, 13-17	Luke 20:27-38

Weekdays, Year One

Monday	Neh. 9:1-25	Rev. 18:1-8	Matt. 15:1-20
Tuesday	Neh. 9:26-38	Rev. 18:9-20	Matt. 15:21-28
Wednesday	Neh. 5:1-19	Rev. 18:21-24	Matt. 15:29-39
Thursday	Neh. 6:1-19 or 1 Macc. 1:1-28	Rev. 19:1-10	Matt. 16:1-12
Friday	Neh. 12:27-47 or 1 Macc. 1:41-63	Rev. 19:11-16	Matt. 16:13-20
Saturday	Neh. 13:1-30 or 1 Macc. 2:1-28	Rev. 20:1-6	Matt. 16:21-28

Weekdays, Year Two

Monday	Joel 1:1-14	Rev. 18:15-24	Luke 14:12-24
Tuesday	Joel 1:15–2:11	Rev. 19:1-10	Luke 14:25-35

Wednesday	Joel 2:12-20	Rev. 19:11-21	Luke 15:1-10
Thursday	Joel 2:21-27	James 1:1-15	Luke 15:1-2, 11-32
Friday	Joel 2:28–3:8	James 1:16-27	Luke 16:1-9
Saturday	Joel 3:9-21	James 2:1-13	Luke 16:10-17

SUNDAY BETWEEN NOVEMBER 13 and 19, inclusive

Sunday A	Judges 4:1-7	1 Thess. 5:1-11	Matt. 25:14-30
B	1 Sam. 1:4-20	Heb. 10:11-25	Mark 13:1-8
C	Isa. 65:17-25	2 Thess. 3:6-13	Luke 21:5-19

Weekdays, Year One

Monday	2 Chron. 23:16-21 or 1 Macc. 3:1-24	Rev. 20:7-15	Matt. 17:1-13
Tuesday	2 Chron. 24:1-19 or 1 Macc. 3:25-41	Rev. 21:1-8	Matt. 17:14-21
Wednesday	2 Chron. 24:20-27 or 1 Macc. 3:42-60	Rev. 21:9-21	Matt. 17:22-27
Thursday	2 Chron. 25:1-19 or 1 Macc. 4:1-25	Rev. 21:22–22:5	Matt. 18:1-9
Friday	2 Chron. 25:20–26:10 or 1 Macc. 4:36-59	Rev. 22:6-13	Matt. 18:10-20
Saturday	2 Chron. 26:11-22	Rev. 22:14-21	Matt. 18:21-35

Weekdays, Year Two

Monday	Hab. 1:1–2:11	James 2:14-26	Luke 16:19-31
Tuesday	Hab. 2:12–3:19	James 3:1-12	Luke 17:1-10
Wednesday	Mal. 1:1, 6-14	James 3:13–4:12	Luke 17:11-19
Thursday	Mal. 2:1-16	James 4:13–5:6	Luke 17:20-37
Friday	Mal. 3:1-12	James 5:7-12	Luke 18:1-8
Saturday	Mal. 3:13–4:6	James 5:13-20	Luke 18:9-14

CHRIST THE KING (or, THE REIGN OF CHRIST)
SUNDAY BETWEEN NOVEMBER 20 and 26, inclusive

On this day, the final Sunday prior to Advent, the church summarizes the teachings about Christ's reign found in recent Sunday readings, and at the same times anticipates the righteous future to be affirmed during Advent. We note the uniqueness of a monarch who comes in great humility, who suffers and dies for the sake of the people.

Sunday A	Ezek. 34:11-16, 20-24	Eph. 1:15-23	Matt. 25:31-46
B	2 Sam. 23:1-7	Rev. 1:4b-8	John 18:33-37
C	Jer. 23:1-6	Col. 1:11-20	Luke 23:33-43

Weekdays, Year One

Monday	Joel 3:1-2, 9-17	1 Pet. 1:1-12	Matt. 19:1-12
Tuesday	Nahum 1:1-13	1 Pet. 1:13-25	Matt. 19:13-22
Wednesday	Obadiah 15-21	1 Pet. 2:1-10	Matt. 19:23-30
Thursday	Zeph. 3:1-13	1 Pet. 2:11-25	Matt. 20:1-16
Friday	Isa. 24:14-23	1 Pet. 3:13–4:6	Matt. 20:17-28
Saturday	Micah 7:11-20	1 Pet. 4:7-19	Matt. 20:29-34

Weekdays, Year Two

Monday	Zech. 10:1-12	Gal. 6:1-10	Luke 18:15-30
Tuesday	Zech. 11:1-17	1 Cor. 3:10-23	Luke 18:31-43
Wednesday	Zech. 12:1-14	Eph. 1:3-14	Luke 19:1-10
Thursday	Zech. 13:1-9	Eph. 1:15-23	Luke 19:11-27
Friday	Zech. 14:1-11	Rom. 15:7-13	Luke 19:28-40
Saturday	Zech. 14:12-21	Phil. 2:1-11	Luke 19:41-48